T0067054

START

TO

FINISH

Mark Dawson

START
TO
FINISH

Mark Dance

START

TO

FINISH

The Pastor's Guide to Leading
a Resilient Life and Ministry

B&H
PUBLISHING
BRENTWOOD, TENNESSEE

978-1-0877-8323-9

Published by B&H Publishing Group
Brentwood, Tennessee

Dewey Decimal Classification: 253
Subject Heading: PASTORAL THEOLOGY
\ CLERGY \ CHRISTIAN LIFE

Cover design and illustration by Darren Welch Design.
Runner image by GrapeImages/istock.

1 2 3 4 5 6 • 27 26 25 24 23

To my parents Ken and Bobbie Dance for showing
me how to love Jesus and His Bride, as well as my own.
This book is an extension of your legacy.

All of the author's royalties and proceeds from this book go to the support of Mission:Dignity, a ministry of GuideStone that enables retirement aged ministers and spouses to live out their days with dignity and security. Mission:Dignity helps more than 2,500 individuals each year with extra money needed for housing, food, and vital medications.

"It reminds them their Southern Baptist family has not forgotten their service to the Lord and His people," GuideStone President Hance Dilbeck said.

To give, to apply for assistance, or to refer someone in need, visit MissionDignity.org or call 877-888-9409. One hundred percent of all gifts to Mission:Dignity assist retirement-aged ministers and/or widows.

ACKNOWLEDGMENTS

I want to thank my wife, Janet, for encouraging me throughout the long journey of writing and publishing this book. She has not only cheered me as I pastored our family, churches, and pastors, but Janet has also ministered alongside me at 100-plus marriage events for ministry couples.

Early in this project, I recruited the help of Dr. Philip Nation. He is an accomplished pastor, writer, and close friend who shares my ambitious goal of helping ministry leaders start and finish well. Philip's encouraging heart and academic mind made this book so much better than it would have been without his help.

Finally, I want to thank Drs. Hance Dilbeck and David Ferguson. Thank you for entrusting me with your legacy ministries at GuideStone and Care4Pastors.

CONTENTS

FOREWORD

The biathlon fascinates me. Every four years, when the winter Olympics roll around, I love watching those amazing athletes compete. The men ski 20 kilometers (12-plus miles) and the women 15 kilometers (9-plus miles), each while carrying a 7-pound rifle. They stop twenty times to shoot at a 2-inch target half a football field away. I am fascinated by the combination of skill, accuracy, and endurance. It is not enough to hit the targets, nor is it sufficient to win the race. They must hit the targets *and* finish the race.

The biathlon is an apt metaphor for the life of a Christian minister. We live under daily demands to be on-target. We live under pressure to be right and to do right in every circumstance and occasion, in season and out of season. In fact, the concentric circles of a target remind us of the ever-present demands—right with God, right with self, right with family, right with church, right with neighbors. We must hit spiritual health, physical health, and mental health targets; not to mention financial, emotional, relational, and vocational targets.

Like the biathlete, the pastor must be on-target over the long haul. We might hit the targets through most of the race, but if we grow too exhausted to finish, it's just target practice. DNF—Did Not Finish—is the fear of everyone who begins the competition. Even worse would be disqualification!

We must be on target over the long haul.

The balance of the biathlon is on display in Paul's admonition to Timothy. "Pay close attention to your life and your teaching; persevere in these things, for in doing this you will save both yourself and your hearers" (1 Tim. 4:16). We must be on target and we must preserve to the finish. This is indeed a high calling.

When the Lord opened the door for me to serve at GuideStone Financial Resources, I understood it as an opportunity to help pastors, missionaries, and ministers Finish Well. We enhance financial security and resilience for those who serve the Lord so that every servant of Christ might finish well. Financial wellness is one part of the whole. To serve well we must be well. Wellness is spiritual, physical, emotional, relational, financial, and vocational. The elements are woven together like a fabric. A flaw in one part will damage the whole.

I asked Mark Dance to come and help me because he has a passion to help ministers be well and serve well. Pastoral wellness is his life's work. He is uniquely prepared to write this book.

Start to Finish—I love that title. It speaks to Intent. One does not finish well on accident. We do not stumble to the finish line; we stride toward it. In kingdom ministry, we must build boundaries, set priorities, keep patterns, establish rhythms that will allow us to "persevere in these things." To finish well, we must start well, serve well, and stay well.

This is a book about intentionality and authenticity.

Mark Dance has accurately concluded that a minister might fake it for a season, but eventually his heart will show. "Guard your heart above all else, for it is the source of life" (Prov. 4:23). The Great Commandment is the foundation for our ministries, as well as our lives. It might not be easy, but it is simple, wonderfully simple. Love the Lord with all your heart, soul, mind ,and strength. One cannot hope to build a sound ministry if he does not live a healthy life. Eventually, your heart shows. I believe that is not just a warning but a promise.

If you have picked up this book, you want to finish well. I have a good word for you.

"Now may the God of peace, who brought up from the dead our Lord Jesus—the great Shepherd of the sheep—through the blood of the everlasting covenant, equip you with everything good to do his will, working in us what is pleasing in his sight, through Jesus Christ, to whom be glory forever and ever. Amen" (Heb. 13:20–21).

Dr. Hance Dilbeck
President/CEO, GuideStone Financial Resources

INTRODUCTION

I will never forget the day when my friend Craig Miller and I drove all day through the hot Jordanian desert at 95 miles per hour to deliver cash and encouragement to embedded SBC missionaries in Baghdad. These heroic missionaries were working alongside the equally heroic U.S. military to replace water pumps in the immediate aftermath of the Iraqi War.

But the war wasn't over. Not even close.

Craig and I only heard the part of President George W. Bush's speech that we wanted to hear a couple of weeks before. "In the battle of Iraq, the major phase of combat is over. The United States and our allies have prevailed," Bush said while standing on the enormous flight deck of the USS *Abraham Lincoln*. He landed on that battleship in an S-3 Viking jet, wearing a flight suit. That was May 2, 2003. I think our country needed President Bush's Texas swagger at that time in our nation's history.

If we had listened carefully to the rest of his speech, Craig and I would have heard Bush say there is still "difficult work to do. Parts of that country remain dangerous . . . there are still Iraqi leaders who must be brought to justice like Saddam Hussein. The al-Qaida terrorist organization is wounded, not destroyed."[1]

Once we arrived, it became obvious that Baghdad was still a very active war zone. Craig and I saw firefights almost every day; the most active one was on our last day in the United Nations building, which was destroyed soon after by a suicide bomber. In a separate attack in traffic, three of the brave IMB missionaries we worked with were killed a few months later.

Pastors, missionaries, and other ministry leaders live and fight daily in an active war zone that is just as real as what we experienced in Baghdad.

In some ways pastors are dealing with even more insidious enemies because their battle, for the most part, is invisible. The world, Satan, and our own flesh conspire against us every day, making it harder and harder to win.

Although our ultimate victory has already been won through Jesus's finished work on the cross, our wounded enemy is shrewdly taking aim at the commissioned officers of the church. Jesus warned us of our enemies' schemes:

> "Tonight all of you will fall away because of me,
> for it is written: 'I will strike the shepherd, and
> the sheep of the flock will be scattered.'" (Matt.
> 26:31)

Sometimes our worst enemy is the person in the mirror. No right-minded minister ever woke up thinking, *How can I blow up my ministry today?* Yet the recent epidemic of messy exits ranges from slow-fading burnouts to epic moral failures.

Sadly, in the three churches I have pastored over the last three decades, I have yet to witness an immediate predecessor or successor finish well. All were terminated, most of them for moral failures. Even the two interim pastorates I have led came on the heels of terminations. It is sad for me to write that fact, and I'm sure it is hard for you to read it.

God has a much better plan for our lives and ministries! He has called us to both start well and finish well: "I am sure of this, that he who started a good work in you will carry it on to completion until the day of Christ Jesus" (Phil. 1:6).

The apostle Paul was a strong finisher. On his last ministry lap, he shared his resolve with his ministry team from Ephesus, "My purpose is to finish my course and the ministry I received from the Lord Jesus" (Acts 20:24). His follow-up letter from death row to Timothy was a legacy statement: "I have fought the good fight, I have finished the race, I have kept the faith" (2 Tim. 4:7).

Our legacy will be determined more by how we finish our race than how we started it, although both are important and connected. **The primary purpose of this book is to help pastors and ministry leaders both start and finish well.** Your war is not yet over, and your race is not yet complete, so thank you for letting me help you press on all the way to the finish line. The fact that you're even reading this book is evidence that you are refusing to coast in casually.

Don't get me wrong—most pastors are not quitters. Our tribe is tough! You can ignore the scary stats we have all heard for years like this: *1,700 pastors leave the ministry every month.*[2] That annoying myth originated in a seminary straw poll that was taken when Roger Staubach was still throwing spirals for the Dallas Cowboys in the '70s.

In September 2015, a groundbreaking Lifeway Research survey of evangelical pastors found that only 1.3 percent abandon the pulpit each year (250, not 1,700). Many of those exits were healthy transitions to other ministries or retirement.[3]

Some pundits predicted that pastors would bail on ministry during the pandemic in 2020–21, but Lifeway's follow-up study in 2022 found the attrition rate had hardly changed at all (1.5%). Although 63 percent said they were overwhelmed by the pandemic, there was no indication that they were bailing on their people.[4]

Most of us who start in ministry will finish in ministry, but is that bar high enough? What if we set the trajectory of our lives, families, and ministries to finish sprinting instead of merely limping across the finish line? When we win, others in our family and ministry win. When we lose, the collateral damage is often bigger than we will ever see in our lifetimes.

> Pay close attention to your life and your teach-
> ing; persevere in these things, for in doing this
> you will save both yourselves and your hearers.
> (1 Tim. 4:16)

I wrote this book from the perspective of a pastor to other pastors, although I realize that many men and women who read this will never use that title. Some of you are pursuing your high calling as an elder, missionary, deacon, teacher, or ministry spouse, which is no less sacred or important. This book is for you as well. You want to finish your ministry stronger than you started it and to do that you must be a resilient, Great Commandment leader.

Some of you are future ministry leaders who will use this book as a discipleship tool. As of this writing, a draft of it is being used as a mentoring manual in more than 100 Ministry Pipeline cohorts throughout Oklahoma for young men and women who have said "yes" to God's call to the ministry. Every disciple-maker needs to be discipled, which does not happen in solitude. So, consider reading it along with at least one other person who has or will assume a ministry leadership role.

Thank you for taking this journey with me.

Lead on!
Mark Dance, DMin
Dallas, Texas

CHAPTER 1

THE MAIN THING

Perhaps the most common church axiom of the 1980s was, "We need to keep the main thing the main thing." I originally liked the ring of it, but apparently so did everyone else, so it became overused and now just comes across as cheesy. I heard it again four days ago at an event that I was speaking at. Make it stop![1]

Over the years I have noticed that "the main thing" is not always the same thing for each speaker. This created a dilemma for me as a young pastor because some boldly declared that evangelism was the main thing, while others insisted it was preaching, discipleship, fellowship, worship, or some ministry project.

The mystery was solved for me about a decade ago when I stumbled across a very familiar passage of Scripture. You may remember when a well-meaning scribe bluntly asked Jesus what the main thing was. Jesus's answer was both refreshingly simple and eternally profound.

> One of the scribes approached. When he heard them debating and saw that Jesus answered them well, he asked him, "Which command is the most important of all?"
>
> Jesus answered, "The most important is 'Listen, Israel! The Lord our God, the Lord is one. Love the Lord your God with all your heart, with all your soul, with all your mind, and with all your strength.' The second is, 'Love your neighbor as yourself.' There is no other command greater than these." (Mark 12:28–31)

This scribe already knew the answer to his own question. I assume most of you also recognize the significance of the Shema (Deut. 6:4–9). Moses instructed faithful Jews 3,500 years ago to write it on their gates and doorposts, and even quote it at the beginning and end of each day. Still today, some orthodox Jews bind a tiny wooden box on their foreheads that contains a written copy of the Shema (Great Commandment) so they will not forget its preeminence.

Jesus said the Shema is the most important text in the Bible (Mark 12:29), which means there is no debate or confusion over what "the main thing" really is for any believer, much less any pastor, missionary, or church leader.

These two "most important" commandments in the Bible are the primary focus of this book because Jesus taught that the whole Bible hangs on the Great Commandments (Matt. 22:40), as do our lives and ministries.

In this book we will unwrap the implications of a Great Commandment life, which is intrinsically connected to a Great Commission ministry.

To pastors and ministry leaders, this is really no secret at all. There are no secrets or shortcuts to pastoral health and resilience. We have all witnessed stellar examples of those who have started and finished well, and we all have friends who have disqualified themselves from ministry.

This book is a summary of my ministry goal to help you start well, serve well, and finish well. A strong finish won't happen tomorrow unless you are willing to own your decisions today. I will be sharing some of my bad decisions in this book, all of which I had to own before I fixed.

Great Commandment leaders have learned to lead themselves first (1 Tim. 4:16) and consequently are leading (*managing*) their families and ministries well.

Please do not blow past the Great Commandments because they're familiar. Allow me to show you how your life and ministry can be strengthened, or even saved, by these two simple, radical old-school precepts. This book is divided into two sections based on each Great Commandment.

LOVING GOD

We will start by focusing on Jesus's first command to love God because he is our "first" love (a.k.a. our "main thing"). Our Lord makes it crystal clear that there is not a more important thing we can do in our day or our whole life than love him with all our heart, soul, mind, and strength. His preeminence in our lives and ministries is a consistent theme throughout Scripture. You will see how this looks for the twenty-first-century Christian pastor. Without him we can do nothing, and through him we can discover the ultimate contentment in his ministry assignments (John 15:5; Phil. 4:13).

LOVING OTHERS

The second half of the book focuses on the command to love our neighbors—those whom God has placed in our lives. The term *neighbor* gives us a hint where to start because it means "nearest one." My nearest one is my wife, Janet.

The Great Commandments not only show us how to love best, but who to love most.

Everyone is equal in God's sight, but as you know, we are not God. My prayer for this section is that you will see God's divine order for your life so that you can boldly protect it.

A CLOSER LOOK

This nameless scribe mentioned earlier was a Pharisee and a member of the Sanhedrin. He was sent to get evidence of heresy to use later at Jesus's trial (Matt. 22:35). Mark's version, however, reveals his personal motives to be genuine when he asked Jesus what the main thing in Scripture was.

The religious elite in Jerusalem made up extra laws instead of following the actual Scripture, then subcategorized them into affirmative and negative groups (248 affirmative laws, 365 negative laws). These rules were also subdivided into heavy and light. The heavy ones were absolutely binding, and the light ones less binding.

Before we can fully understand and apply the first and greatest commandment, there are five key terms in it, which we need to explore and clarify: *Lord, first, greatest, love,* and *all.* Each term speaks to our relationship priorities.

"Lord" (Yahweh)

There are so many wonderful names for God in the Bible, but only one covenant name—Yahweh/Jehovah. Ancient Hebrew had no vowels, so a more accurate English translation would be *YHWH.* Out of respect for the personal name of God, it remained unpronounced for centuries, so we will not really know how to accurately pronounce it on this side of heaven.

The proper name of the one true God means "self-existent or eternal; the existing one." Jesus's name in Hebrew was Joshua (y'shua), which means "Yahweh is salvation."

I love that we cannot say Jesus's name without also saying Yahweh!

It is very important to God, and should be to us, that we not take His name in vain. It is the third of the Ten Commandments, only preceded by commands forbidding other gods or graven images. These first three commands are like a no-compete clause in our covenant. God insists on being our "main thing." This is why getting his name right is so important.

"most important," or "first" (protos)

The scribe asked, "Which command is the most important of all?" (Mark 12:28). The Greek word *protos* is typically translated as "most important." The KJV, though, translates it as "first." One thing I like about the use of "first" is that it speaks to the priority of loving God. Also, Jesus used "second" to refer to the other great commandment: *Love your neighbor as yourself.* The closer I look at Scripture, the more I see an emerging pecking order for our lives and ministries.

My life and ministry have never been the same since God seared into my heart the powerful simplicity of making Jesus my first love. This truth made a great impact on me as a pastor after I reluctantly admitted to myself that my first love was no longer my first priority.

Many Bible translations use "most important" because it more accurately captures the weight of the scribe's question. The expert in the law wanted to know the priority of the commands, not merely the sequence of them. If we miss the first command (loving God completely) and fulfill the second command (loving our neighbor), then we are left with mere humanism. Our neighbors are vitally important, but they are not equally important as Jesus.

Christ reminds us that *the most important* thing we will do today, or any day of our lives, is to love him.

We know intuitively that God is more important than anyone or anything else in creation. *Shema* is Hebrew for "hear," since the Shema begins with, "Hear [listen], O Israel" (Deut. 6:4 ESV).

This clear covenant commitment to God reinforces the first two of the Ten Commandments, which forbid other gods and idols. You don't have to be a numerologist to see how the Bible repeatedly affirms there is only **one** God, and he demands the first and most important place in our lives.

God did not leave room for anyone or anything else on his throne. The terms of God's covenant are for Jesus to be our *only* Lord. He is the Savior and the primary hero of human history—and of his church. Pastor, you don't have to be the hero; that job belongs to Christ.

"greatest" (megas)

After Jesus answered the scribe's initial question, he reinforced his answer with an even stronger term: *greatest*. Jesus said, "There is no other command **greater** than these" (Mark 12:31, emphasis mine). Both terms are also used in Matthew's version of this conversation. It reads, "'Love the Lord your God. . . .' This is the **greatest** [*megas*] and most important [*protos*] command" (Matt. 22:37–38, emphasis mine).

God used the combined strength of these two terms—*protos* and *megas*—to grab my attention in an intensely personal way in 2006. I had been fasting and praying for several days in a quiet mountain cabin in Jasper, Arkansas. I do not enjoy fasting, but it is one of the best ways to cure my spiritual attention deficit disorder. After almost two decades of pastoring, I was ripe for a fresh encounter with the Lord.

I look at this experience as my "face mask moment" with God. When I was a teenager, my football coaches would sometimes grab our helmet face masks to get our undivided attention. It always worked! Although God was gentler than my football coaches, I left that cabin knowing what my game plan was going to be for the rest of my life and ministry. It was in that Ozark Mountain cabin that the Great Commandment was freshly seared into my mind, and I pray you will have a similar experience as you read this book. I hope it will help sharpen the focus of those who are preparing for a lifetime of ministry, as well as those who are striving to finish their ministry well.

No ministry leader who strives to start or finish well will ignore or neglect the top two priorities that God commanded, Moses authored, and Jesus reinforced.

"love" (agapaō)

In 2003, Campus Crusade for Christ founder Bill Bright hosted a breakfast in his Orlando home for a few of my Arkansas pastor friends, which included Rick Bezet and Bill Elliff. You cannot imagine how excited I was about the opportunity to meet this ministry titan in his own home!

His lovely wife, Vonette, served us breakfast while Dr. Bright encouraged us greatly in the Lord. His breaths were measured because he was connected to oxygen tubes, with the tank behind his wheelchair. Before we left, Dr. Bright gave us an autographed copy of his book *First Love: Renewing Your Passion for God*. In it he says this about the Great Commandment: "I do not believe there is any issue more crucial for you and me to consider in this life."[2] This would be his last book. Dr. Bright finished his earthly race a few short months later. His love for the Great Commission and the Great Commandments lives on through pastors and leaders like you and me.

The title of Dr. Bright's book, *First Love*, came from a passage of Scripture addressed to a young church in Ephesus. This church had many things going for them like solid doctrine, discipline, and endurance. But at the end of the day, Jesus called them out for neglecting and abandoning their first love. Jesus wrote a letter to them saying,

> "You have abandoned the love you had at first.
> Remember then how far you have fallen; repent,
> and do the works you did at first." (Rev. 2:4–5a)

As a ministry leader, you are likely already familiar with the Greek word for *love* used here: *agapaō*. Jesus used this same term in the Great Commandments. *Agapaō* describes a covenant love that is based on grace, not performance. It is a love that distinguishes Christianity from all other world religions because of its one-sidedness. Jesus paid for a freedom that we did not earn or deserve. We committed the crime, and he paid the penalty. His *agapaō* love is an extension of God's mercy and grace through his work of redemption.

There is no other religion with those terms. To experience this divine love is to experience the pinnacle of all relationships. Agapaō is what makes the Great Commandment great. This love is central to our most important command. The love of Jesus is free and unconditional, yet it is expensive and evokes a radical response. It is at once personal and universal.

When I attempt to explain the love of God, my words seem to fall short and shallow. But I know that it is Christ's love that compels us to engage in ministry (2 Cor. 5:14). It is the very source for our new life and our calling. Nothing fuels us more than knowing God's love. Every other motivation is short-lived and comparatively empty.

I am praying for your experience with this book to be more than a mere academic exercise. I want you to do more than understand this great love. I am praying for you to "know Christ's love that surpasses knowledge, so that you may be filled with all the fullness of God" (Eph. 3:19).

Pastor, I want to invite you into the deepest part of the faith pool. My hope is that your growing love for Jesus will overflow into the other priority relationships we will explore in the second section of this book.

"all" (holos)

The first hockey game I ever attended was in 2016. The game was only a few blocks from the Lifeway office I had at that time in downtown Nashville. I had an opportunity to get a ticket for half-price, so I went for it, although I honestly had no idea what I was getting into.

My first game was not only a professional NHL game, but it was also a first-round playoff game! The Nashville Predators were playing the Anaheim Ducks, and I got sucked into the series as well as the sport. The Preds lost that game but won the series and went to the seventh game in the second-round divisional playoffs before getting knocked out by the San Jose Sharks, who eventually won the Stanley Cup that year. The next year the Preds played in their first Stanley Cup, and I took my son and son-in-law to one of those playoff games. I am now officially a hockey fan!

"Fan" is short for "fanatic," which implies that you are behind your team 100 percent, or all-in. The Shema is basically asking if we are *all*-in for God:

> "Love the Lord your God with *all* your heart,
> with *all* your soul, with *all* your mind, and with
> *all* your strength." (Mark 12:30, emphasis mine)

Athletes and fans are not hesitant about going all-in. Neither are people who love their hobbies, politics, or careers. Should Jesus expect anything less from the leaders of his church?

Jesus, our first love, desires and even requires *all* from us. He reciprocates generously, so don't be afraid of jumping into the deep end of his unconditional love. Jesus is asking for all your life, all your love, and all your priorities to be set on him.

Dr. David Ferguson said it well in his landmark book *The Great Commandment Principle*: "The Great Commission is what we do, but the Great Commandment embodies who we are. We cannot effectively do what we have been called to do unless we embrace who we have been called to be."[3]

The scribe whose question prompted Jesus to quote the Great Commandment was himself an expert on the Old Testament Scriptures. An academic assistant to the power players, he was also an attorney, a professor, and parliamentarian. His question was preceded by several salty attempts to discredit Jesus by the

Pharisees, Sadducees, and Herodians, yet this scribe was sincerely seeking truth.

> Then the scribe said to him, "You are right, teacher. You have correctly said that he is one, and there is no one else except him. And to love him with all your heart, with all your understanding, and with all your strength, and to love your neighbor as yourself, is far more important than all the burnt offerings and sacrifices."
>
> When Jesus saw that he answered wisely, he said to him, "You are not far from the kingdom of God." And no one dared to question him any longer. (Mark 12:32–34)

The crowd of skeptics was silenced by the truth Jesus stated and by the scribe's response. It is an interaction that we need repeated in our own lives. Pastor, you likely don't have a crowd waiting for you to give such an answer, but you do have the God of heaven waiting to see where you will place your allegiance. You have a community of people waiting to see how you will prioritize your life and ministry.

The bottom line is that healthy churches are led by healthy pastors who love God with all their heart, soul, mind, and strength. I want to invite you to spend the next few minutes asking God to help you love him first. Then spend a few more minutes in worship loving him with all your heart, soul, mind, and strength. There is nothing more important you will do today.

> "It's not so important who starts the game but who finishes it."[4]

CHAPTER 2

A 4D LOVE

recently bought my first 4K television. Let me tell you. It. Is. Awesome!

4K has some of the highest resolution in televisions, and it has been around long enough to be affordable and standard on most new TVs. The term *4K* describes the resolution of the TV set by the number of pixels used to create an image.

Some might think, *That dude has arrived . . .* I would argue against that point if I had not already enthusiastically accepted my scepter (remote control). Some 3K curmudgeon will probably point out that technology will eventually evolve beyond my new graven image to a 5K, but nobody can rob me of my temporary technological triumph!

My TV rocks because the extra resolution of a 4K screen adds more detail, depth, and color resolution to the picture. The images appear more lifelike. It is incredible. The 4K screens have about 8 million pixels, which is around four times what a 1080p set can display. I don't really understand technology, but my ignorance is bliss at this point because I am as happy as a boy with a new toy.

In this chapter, I will attempt to explain the Great Commandment love of God with an even greater measure of bliss than my television. I pray that it will help you to enjoy your relationship with God on a level that exceeds your understanding of it. The mystery of our relationship with God can become more defined than ever before. We can move from blurry attempts to reveal our allegiance to defined actions that reveal a heart fully set on God.

In Jesus's command for us to love God, he spoke of four dimensions in our lives. Each of these dimensions is a particular part of who you are. When we read them together in the context of Jesus's great commands, you can see that he is talking about loving God with your whole life. Jesus wants the total package of who you are.

I've spent more hours than I can count trying to understand then write about these four dimensions (4D) of loving God: *heart*, *soul*, *mind*, and *strength*. I cannot be casual about interpreting any passage of Scripture, which is especially true of the *most important* one! At the end of the day, we all want the love of God to define who we are as people as well as pastors.

Now, let's dig into what it means to have a 4D love for God!

AN INTEGRATED LOVE

As students and teachers of God's Word, it will be helpful for us to build a strong theological foundation for the greatest commandment in the Bible. We will start by taking the time in this chapter to understand all four dimensions of our lives: *heart, soul, mind,* and *strength.* Each dimension overlaps quite a bit with the others in Scripture, so try not to overanalyze them. Otherwise, all of this will become just another academic exercise, which would be a phenomenal waste of your time. The Shema is a comprehensive covenant, not a compartmentalized one.

We must be careful not to merely exegete and preach about the love of God while failing to give our hearts fully to him. Great Commandment love was never meant to be dissected as information just to be used in a song, sermon, or lesson. It is Jesus's call to himself.

After pastoring for two decades, I lost that idea along the way. In having a fruitful ministry that others called successful, I got caught up in ministry performance and lost the priority of my *first love.* I eventually found myself lonely, confused, and clinically depressed.

As you work through these four dimensions of loving God, do so with a mental mirror so you can see where you may be struggling and ask God how he wants to renew your life and ministry.

Some believe that people have three distinct natures: body, soul, and spirit (tripartite view). Others believe we are made of only two parts: body and spirit (bipartite view). They believe our spirit is the internal part of us (a.k.a. heart/soul), while our bodies make up the external part of us.

At a glance, the first Great Commandment seems to teach a quadripartite view of humans: *heart*, *soul*, *mind*, and *strength*. All four of these are components of your life, not compartments of your life. We don't just have a heart, soul, mind, and body. We are the sum of those things.

These four dimensions were meant to be integrated, not separated into each person's life. Perhaps this explains why they are listed a little differently by each of the gospel writers.

Sometimes there is a clear distinction between the heart, soul, and mind. But much of the time they are used interchangeably in the Bible. Look at 1 Thessalonians 5:23: "Now may the God of peace himself sanctify you completely. And may your whole spirit, soul, and body be kept sound and blameless at the coming of our Lord Jesus Christ." Here Paul uses the phrase "and may your whole . . ." as if he is describing the three dimensions as the summary of a person's being.

God wants all of you. Every part. So let me carefully break down each of the four components of Great Commandment love.

Our HEARTS

God gave every person on the planet a physical heart. It is the organ that keeps our life-giving blood pumping to the rest of our body. Putting it bluntly, without our physical hearts we are physically dead. Likewise, without our spiritual hearts we are spiritually dead.

I can understand why some people get confused by the idea of one person having two hearts. After all, the Bible uses the same words in both Greek (*kardia*) and Hebrew (*lebab*) to describe the physical heart and the spiritual heart. This tends to be even more confusing to concrete-thinking people like me. Our spiritual hearts are the invisible central core of who we are, just as our physical hearts are the central core of our bodies. Without new spiritual hearts we are spiritually dead, but the good news is that Christians get a spiritual heart transplant at the point of their salvation.

Our spiritual hearts became fully redeemed when we surrendered our lives to Jesus. My heart was desperately wicked before Jesus transformed me on June 12, 1980. The moment I cried out to him for salvation, I got a brand-new heart (spirit), which is the reality for all Christians. Since my salvation more than forty years ago, my heart has been undergoing an endless process of sanctification, which is the slow roll to spiritual maturity.

The Bible uses the word *spirit* interchangeably with *heart*. We see this in Ezekiel's use of a common Eastern writing method called parallelism. In this writing or speaking style, the same idea is emphasized by repeating it using different terms.

> Throw off all the transgressions you have committed and get yourselves a new heart [*leb*] and a new spirit [*ruah*]. (Ezek. 18:31)

Since Western thought usually associates the heart with feelings, you might be surprised to find out that the most common Hebrew use of *heart* (*lebab*) is in reference to our thoughts, not our feelings. It is why Jeremiah said, "I will put my teaching within them and write it on their hearts. I will be their God, and they will be my people" (Jer. 31:33b). The same is true of the Greek term (*kardia*), depending on its context.

Our hearts are more than just a place where our thoughts and feelings reside. My heart is who I am, and your heart is who you are. In chapter 3, we will explore how spiritually resilient pastors can love the Lord with all of our hearts.

Our SOULS

The term *soul* is often used as a synonym for the individual person and is often translated in the Christian Standard Bible translation as *life* (used 104 times), or as *person* (used 38 times). All humans—lost or saved—have souls because God has breathed life into us all. Genesis 2:7 states, "Then the LORD God formed the man out of the dust from the ground and breathed the breath of life into his nostrils, and the man became a living being."

There are currently 7.5 billion souls on our planet,[1] and every soul will live forever . . . somewhere. Only two billion of our global neighbors profess to be Christians, so we have so much more work to do to advance the gospel!

The Greek term for soul is *psyche*, from which we get the English word *psychology*. While the heart is the eternal part of our lives that is fully redeemed, the soul is the internal part of us that is constantly being restored and renewed. The terms *soul* and *spirit* are used as metaphors for breath and wind in both Hebrew and Greek. The Hebrew term for soul (*nephesh*; breathing creature) refers to our physical life, which God has given to all of us.

> "The life [soul] of every living thing is in his hand, as well as the breath [physical] of all humanity." (Job 12:10)

Every human soul is valuable and made in the image of God, yet with a unique personality. Some assume that their soul will take prominence in the afterlife. But your soul is your life right now . . . today. Perhaps this assumption comes from this commonly misinterpreted Bible passage about the soul: "For what is a man profited, if he shall gain the whole world, and lose his own soul? Or what shall a man give in exchange for his soul?" (Matt. 16:26 KJV).

Most translations, like the Christian Standard Bible, translate the term *psyche* as "life" instead of "soul." This passage in Matthew 16 is not talking about losing your eternal salvation, it is talking about losing yourself in this earthly life. Your soul is your life, and you must entrust your soul to your Savior daily for your sanctification.

Is it well with your soul? Does your interior life need some rearranging? In chapter 4, we will further pursue what it means to be an emotionally healthy leader who loves God with all your soul.

Our MINDS

The term *mind* was not in the original Shema that Moses spoke and wrote. Perhaps this is because the Hebrews made no real distinction between the heart and the mind. They believed that our hearts are where the real thinking happens. I assume that Jesus added *mind* to his recitation of the Shema because the Greco-Roman culture that his followers were born into viewed the mind as the place from which our thoughts originated. Our current Western culture assumes the same. At the end of the day, we see very little difference in Scripture between a person's mind and heart.

> Don't worry about anything, but in everything, through prayer and petition with thanksgiving, present your requests to God. And the peace of God, which surpasses all understanding, will guard your *hearts* and *minds* in Christ Jesus. (Phil. 4:6–7, emphasis mine)

God still promises to guard the hearts and minds of those who love him. Mental health is no less important than physical, spiritual, or emotional health, so in chapter 5, we will explore practical ways to love Jesus with all our minds.

Our STRENGTH

In my opinion, *strength* is primarily a reference to the strength of our physical bodies. This Greek term (*ischys*) for strength can mean will, might, force, or power. The Hebrew equivalent (*koah*) refers to a person's physical energy.

Perhaps you have noticed that ministry takes a lot of energy. Sometimes, I don't know whether I feel drained physically, mentally, or emotionally—I just know I'm exhausted. Even as I type this, my voice is completely gone. I lost it on a Saturday and had to tag in a pastor on my staff to preach my sermon. I was tempted to power through on Sunday morning, but my wise wife talked me off of that silly ledge.

We all want to glorify God with our bodies and love him with all our strength. King Josiah apparently figured it out, and so can we:

> Before him there was no king like him who
> turned to the LORD with all his *heart* and with
> all his *soul* and with all his *strength* according to
> all the law of Moses, and no one like him arose
> after him. (2 Kings 23:25, emphasis mine)

Physical health is often the last thing that ministry leaders feel like they have time to manage. We even have well-meaning sayings like, "I'd rather burn out than rust out." Some pastors wear self-neglect as a badge of honor. In chapter 6, we will explore how healthy leaders can grow in their love for God and others with all their strength by leading a healthy life.

BUCKLE UP!

In some ways I understand 4D physics and 4K technology even more than I understand the mysterious nuances of my four-dimensional love for God. My limited understanding of these four dimensions of Great Commandment love has become much more than a book project to me. This has been a literal labor of love!

> I pray that you, being rooted and firmly established in love, may be able to comprehend with all the saints what is the length and width, height and depth of God's love, and to know Christ's love that surpasses knowledge, so that you may be filled with all the fullness of God. (Eph. 3:17–19)

CHAPTER 3

WITH ALL MY HEART

My annual physical exam was yesterday, which started with my heart. A nurse checked my heartbeat with a stethoscope, and someone else took my blood pressure. After I was told my blood pressure was "perfect," I got an EKG that verified that my heart was working just fine. This was very important information to me since both sides of my family have a concerning history of heart disease.

The overall physical was comprehensive and so the doctor checked the condition of my entire body. My heart got considerably more attention than other organs because it is essential to everything else. Every other part of my body depends on the health of my heart, so God put it at the center of the body and placed it in a cage made of bone.

The Great Commandment specifically mentions how important our hearts are to God's heart.

> "Listen, Israel: The LORD our God, the LORD
> is one. Love the LORD your God with *all your
> heart*, with all your soul, and with all your
> strength. These words that I am giving you
> today are to be *in your heart*." (Deut. 6:4–6,
> emphasis mine)

I think it is interesting that Moses introduced the Shema immediately after introducing the Ten Commandments in Deuteronomy. The Lord did not want the Hebrews to have the Shema as a mere religious exercise to be observed periodically. His intention is that it will be at the core of your very being.

Your heart is like the operating system of a computer—the core program that makes all of the other programs function. Without the operating system, your computer is just a block of circuits that cannot do anything. The Great Commandment needs to be uploaded to the hard drive of our hearts. Only then will we lead our lives, families, and ministries well.

The Great Commandment is our Great Physician's comprehensive check-up for the hearts of pastors. It compels us to answer this important question: ***Am I loving God with all my heart?***

Don't rush past that question. If you cannot confidently say "yes," I pray that God will use this book—but specifically this chapter—to help you to return to your *first love* with the abandoned enthusiasm of a pastor ready to love God completely with his heart.

A SPIRITUAL EKG

The EKG I got during that annual exam was a "snapshot" of the electrical activity of my heart. The test checked my heart's rhythm. My doctor wanted to know if it was beating in its intended rhythm. When the heart beats too fast, too slow, or with a skipping, irregular rhythm, the person has an arrhythmia, which is dangerous to our total body. EKGs can also show whether our heart is injured, at risk, or unhealthy.

Today's spiritual checkup may save you from a spiritual heartache, spiritual atrophy, or even spiritual death if you discover you have not been born again. Your spiritual heart was created to be in a thriving, loving relationship with your Creator. There is not one thing you will do today more important than walk with God. For that matter, there is not one thing you will do in your home or church this week more important than loving and worshipping God. We lead out of the overflow of that relationship, so I want to stop right here and commend you for reading this far into this book. You obviously want to keep growing and leading well!

How do we test our hearts to see if it is out of rhythm with our Savior? Jesus gave us a spiritual EKG in the form of a parable to assess the condition of our hearts. I want to ask you to read the parable of the sower in Luke 8:4–15 and allow God to use it to diagnose the current spiritual condition of your heart. It presents four kinds of soil showing four potential conditions of our heart.

After you read the parable, answer four very important diagnostic questions listed below.

The parable of the sower is the only parable to appear in all three Synoptic Gospels, which underscores its importance. Jesus often used agriculture metaphors because almost everyone farmed in that culture or at least knew something about it. Even in urban settings, most people have tried to grow something at some point in their lives. In this parable, the sower is God, the seed is His Word, and our hearts are the soil.

To help you assess the condition of your heart, ask yourself, and God, these four diagnostic questions.

IS MY HEART TOO HARD?

> "The sower sows the word. Some are like the word sown on the path. When they hear, immediately Satan comes and takes away the word sown in them." (Mark 4:14–15)

Our hearts are vulnerable to attacks by Satan and demons. On the surface this comes across as fatalistic, but God does not give Satan a blank check. Lucifer is on a leash. We allow ourselves to be bullied by this spiritual blowfish when we forget Jesus's authority over Satan. God allows Satan the latitude to test us so that our faith can be proven as strong or exposed as weak. But it does not eliminate the need for us to assess our own hearts.

This parable is not just about the evil hearts of leaders like Judas Iscariot. Peter and other frontline leaders were constantly in the devil's crosshairs as well. Jesus warned Peter, "Satan has asked to sift you like wheat. But I have prayed for you that your faith may not fail. And you, when you have turned back, strengthen your brothers" (Luke 22:31–32).

We all know what a bad night Peter had immediately after that. Shortly after he fell asleep during an important prayer summit, he whacked off the ear of a temple guard. If that weren't bad enough, he denied even knowing Jesus three times.

Peter was a spiritual champion, but he was clearly exhausted, vulnerable, and in need of some soul care. Brian Croft reflects on a season when he hit a wall and his soul was dying: "We ignore the warning signs of stress, depression, and anxiety that the body so often communicates to us if we listen. We keep pressing on and pressing through—until we hit the wall. Part of embracing our weakness is to know when to run and go and know when to stop and rest."[1]

Some reading this book are being sifted by Satan right now. If your faith has failed like Peter, you can still turn back and strengthen your brothers and sisters. Satan is going to continually attempt to snatch the seed of God's Word from you. Continuing with Peter's story, some of his sifting happened later, because of obedience, not disobedience. Right after James was martyred, Peter was imprisoned. But look at the church's response to Peter's trial:

> Peter was kept in prison, but the church was
> praying fervently to God for him. (Acts 12:5)

As they prayed, the Lord rescued Peter from Herod's henchmen. He was escorted past sixteen armed guards by an angel of the Lord because the church was praying for him. I firmly believe that there would be significantly fewer pastors burning out and dropping out if their churches prayed for them with such passion. As pastors and church leaders, don't be embarrassed to ask for prayer support from your church family. We will likely have only as many intercessors as we recruit.

Healthy, resilient pastors will remind themselves regularly who is really in charge of our churches. We do not have to chase the devil, nor must we allow him to chase us away from our families and ministries. Leaders need to "be sober-minded, be alert. Your adversary the devil is prowling around like a roaring lion, looking for anyone he can devour" (1 Pet. 5:8). No leader needs to be "taken advantage of by Satan . . . [or] ignorant of his schemes" (2 Cor. 2:11).

Jesus had a considerable amount of trouble with the religious leaders in Jerusalem who were "hard hearted." Most faithful Jews not only believed the Great Commandment was important, they quoted it twice a day and wrote it on their doorposts (mezuzahs). As I mentioned already, some even put it in a little box and tied it on their foreheads (phylacteries). Perhaps this formal expression of their love for God was initially helpful, yet God desired for the

Shema to be tattooed on their hearts and expressed with genuine affection (Jer. 31:33; Heb. 8:10).

Pastors must be careful when approaching familiar subjects like this. I am in conversation with pastors, ministers, and missionaries almost every day somewhere on this planet who already know all of the textbook answers to life's deepest questions. This knowledge makes us vulnerable because of our reluctance to assess and guard our hearts. Trusting our hearts (or guts) is dangerous because Jesus taught that our hearts are prone to becoming cesspools of death. He said in Mark 7:21–22,

> "For from within, out of people's hearts, come evil thoughts, sexual immoralities, thefts, murders, adulteries, greed, evil actions, deceit, self-indulgence, envy, slander, pride, and foolishness."

Perhaps like the Ephesians, "You have abandoned the love you had at first" (Rev. 2:4). You know you are saved, but you also know that you have stalled out spiritually. If you can't honestly say that you are all-in like you were at the beginning, Jesus says the next step is to turn it around (repent).

> "Remember then how far you have fallen; repent and do the works you did at first. Otherwise, I will come to you and remove your lampstand from its place, unless you repent." (Rev. 2:5)

If you are currently living and leading on life support, let me remind you that you do not have to stay that way. Restoration and resilience are right on the other side of repentance. Repentance is not easy for those of us with hard heads, hard hearts, and public ministries—but God's grace is much greater than all our sins. If you will take the time at this very moment to hear from God and apply his Word, the enemy will be powerless to take it away from the soil of your hungry heart.

PRAYER: *Jesus, only you can soften my hard heart. I turn from my sin and selfishness to you with a humble heart. I choose to listen for your voice in your Word. I pray that you would deliver me from the evil one and lead me away from temptation today.*

IS MY HEART TOO SHALLOW?

I had more enthusiasm than skill in my very first experience on a sports team. The first-grade basketball team at the YMCA in Tyler, Texas, was led by my close friend, Vandy, who was by far the best player on our team. He could miraculously both shoot and dribble, and I was justifiably jealous because I could do neither. The sum of our team strategy was to give the ball to this alpha first grader.

In my first basketball game, I miraculously stole the ball from the other team and enthusiastically took off toward the goal! I was euphoric about finally getting to dribble the basketball and was surprised at how easy it was to take this turnover and score a lay-up. I assumed I was so fast that nobody could even keep up with me!

Being my first and only score, I was confused by the lack of enthusiasm by my parents, coach, and teammates on the other end of the court. My celebration was unfortunately premature and short-lived because I was enthusiastically running in the wrong direction and scored a goal for the other team!

If our excitement about the Lord is rooted in a religious experience rather than an authentic love relationship, our fire for God will flame out fast. Enthusiasm is usually short-lived, so we must not confuse it with the deep love of God that grows within us in season and out.

Too many conversion experiences happen on shallow soil. Pastors often celebrate the show of hands that shoot up at Vacation Bible School when asked if they want to go to heaven someday. Students rush the altar in response to a compelling camp or concert speaker who tried to literally scare the hell out of them. Adults who experience a brush with death, divorce, or detention are vulnerable to knee-jerk flare prayers as well.

> "And others are like seed sown on rocky ground.
> When they hear the word, immediately they
> receive it with joy. But they have no root; they
> are short-lived. When distress or persecution
> comes because of the word, they immediately
> fall away." (Mark 4:16–17)

In this portion of the parable, the seed withered without moisture because it could not possibly take root in the rocks. Jesus warns us that our joy can quickly turn into apathy when his Word doesn't have a chance to take root and grow in our hearts.

Ministers need to make sure that we don't cheapen the gospel by making it sound like the path of least resistance. Jesus taught quite the opposite (Matt. 7:13–14).

We can also cheapen the gospel by not allowing the Word to take root and grow in our own hearts. Pastors and missionaries are not immune to having a shallow, weak heart. Our tender hearts can easily turn into rocky soil when we neglect to let Jesus shepherd our own hearts.

As pastors, we deal with the same problems as everyone else in our church. It is not unusual for ministry leaders and spouses to struggle with erosion in our marriages, rebellion in our children, and frustration from helping aging parents. We run out of time, money, and energy just like everyone else. If these challenges expose the shallowness of an unguarded heart, quickly go back to the well of grace—both for yourself and for your ministry.

That well of grace is where you will find your healthy heart again. The apostle Paul prays for his Ephesian church to grow deeper in their heart knowledge of Jesus, "to know Christ's love that surpasses knowledge" (Eph. 3:19). Paul uses two different words here to describe knowledge. He is praying that they will *know* (perceive/understand) the love that surpasses *knowledge* (secular facts). Personal, intimate knowledge of Jesus surpasses any cerebral, linear knowledge of God's Word, although both are important for any church leader. You probably already know the answers in your head, but when is the last time you went deeper into the recesses of your heart to recover the joy that Jesus filled you with?

PRAYER: *Jesus, I trust that you can deepen my faith. So much is pressing in to distract me from your love, your Word, and your work. I want to focus my heart's attention on you afresh. Transform my shallow heart into a fertile heart that bears lasting fruit.*

IS MY HEART TOO CLUTTERED?

> "As for the seed that fell among thorns, these are the ones who, when they have heard, go on their way and are choked with worries, riches, and pleasures of life, and produce no mature fruit." (Luke 8:14)

When God's Word competes with our wills, it will expose a cluttered, selfish heart. There are three common culprits of a cluttered heart: worry, wealth, and wants.

Worry

As thorns can choke out healthy plants, so can worries choke out our healthy faith. I'm not talking about losing your faith;

rather I'm talking about losing your joy with a slowly eroding faith.

One close friend who is a pastor once lamented to me, "Sometimes I wonder if my walk with God would be easier if I weren't in the ministry." Yes, even church work can choke out our spiritual growth. Every pastor I know wants their spiritual growth to outpace their ministry growth, but it doesn't always work out that way.

The origin of the English word for worry comes from the German word *wurgen*—which means "to choke." If worry is suffocating your faith, stop now and prayerfully meditate on this passage. Ask God to guard your heart and mind with his peace.

> Don't worry about anything, but in everything,
> through prayer and petition with thanksgiving,
> present your requests to God. And the peace of
> God, which surpasses all understanding, will
> guard your hearts and minds in Christ Jesus.
> (Phil. 4:6–7)

We must intentionally and consistently check our own spiritual pulse. Additionally, we need to ask a couple of mature believers to help us assess the condition of our heart.

Wealth

I was thirteen years old when I heard the news that Elvis died by essentially choking on his wealth. Elvis has sold the most solo albums in history and was nominated fourteen times for Grammys. I have seen his fancy cars and his gold-plated grand piano in the Country Music Hall of Fame in Nashville, as well as Graceland in Memphis. All of his awards, toys, records, fame, and money are a sad reminder of "the deceitfulness of riches," that led to the destructive end of this dear brother in Christ.

None of us are immune to the false sense of security and worth that comes with wealth. Even pastors get caught in the trap. "If my salary was more" and "If the church budget was bigger" are statements that show that our trust is more in riches than in the King. Someday all our stuff will end up in the dump, in storage, or in our kid's garage.

Wants

The Greek term translated "pleasures of life" points to an unquenchable sensual desire. It is also the Greek word from which we get our English word *hedonism*. Hedonism is a belief that pleasure, or worldly happiness, is life's highest goal. Roman emperors were notorious for their hedonism, which became the cultural norm for the Roman Empire.

In the book *This Is Our Time*, Trevin Wax wrote that the biggest myth we surrender to is the pursuit of happiness. A Barna Research project found that 84 percent of Americans believe "the highest goal for life is to enjoy it as much as possible." Sadder still was the fact that 66 percent of churchgoing Christians bought into the same lie![2]

As you well know, hedonism and materialism are alive and well in today's culture and are an ominous threat to our churches and pulpits. Sports, school activities, work, and hobbies often have a stranglehold on our lives. Our obsession with achieving and acquiring leaves our hearts barren, exhausted, and empty.

As pastors, we are tempted to focus on the measurements of ministry success rather than on Jesus. Our egos sometimes crave bigger crowds and more attention, yet our primary motivation should be the love for Christ that drew us to our ministry call in the first place.

PRAYER: *Jesus, I admit that my earthly desires have gotten in the way of my love for you. You are my joy and my salvation. Nothing is as great as serving and loving you. Lord, purify my heart from the worries of this world.*

IS MY HEART HEALTHY?

> "And those like seed sown on good ground hear
> the word, welcome it, and produce fruit thirty,
> sixty, and a hundred times what was sown."
> (Mark 4:20)

I realize that many of you are walking with God consistently and your love for God is growing. You are likely reading this book because you are intentionally investing in your spiritual health. Or perhaps you are reading this book with another pastor or mentor, or maybe with a mentee who is ministering "out of season." If not, perhaps you should be. I know we all have ministry friends who could use a spiritual EKG. We all know of someone who needs a Barnabas to help them get back on their knees again.

When the human heart beats in a normal rhythm, it shares blood with the rest of the body—and all the parts of the body win. Spiritually resilient pastors are normal in God's eyes, because that is his plan for every Christian's life and ministry. Mediocrity is the cultural norm, but it is not the Christian norm. Lukewarm love is abnormal and nauseating to God (Rev. 3:16). A white-hot love for God is not the new normal, it is the old-school normal.

We must refuse accepting any cultural redefinition of Christianity. The Great Commandment is old school. It takes us back more than 2,000 years to the words of Jesus, and 1,500 years even further back to the words of Moses. Of course, all of God's Word originates from the heart of God and is as timeless and relevant today as in any other point in history.

Regardless of your personal diagnosis, the universal prognosis is simple:

> Give me an undivided mind to fear your name.
> I will praise you with all my heart, Lord my
> God. (Ps. 86:11b–12a)

What a privilege it is to know that the Lord of all creation desires a thriving love relationship with us. Although some hearts are hard, shallow, or cluttered, we are only truly responsible for the receptivity of our own heart.

Now that you have taken your spiritual EKG, what is the true condition of your heart today? Is it hard, shallow, and cluttered; or is it receptive, healthy, and fruitful?

If your heart is receptive, and your life and ministry are consequently fruitful, please do not forget that God's love is a gift we neither deserved nor initiated. Otherwise, pride may creep in and steal away some of God's glory as well as our joy.

Once our hearts are healthy again, how do we stay healthy so that we can finish strong some day?

Ray Allen retired from the NBA in 2016 after two titles and ten All-Star appearances. Allen was the all-time 3-point leader with 2,973 points until Steph Curry broke that record on December 14, 2022. In a letter to his younger self, he wrote, "The secret to success in the NBA is there is no secret. It's just boring old habits."[3]

No secrets.

No shortcuts.

Just walk with God every day and let him cultivate your heart until it stops beating.

CHAPTER 4

WITH ALL MY SOUL

After eleven hours in the morgue, ninety-one-year-old Janina Kolkiewicz woke up and started stirring around. She had been declared dead by her physician in an eastern Polish town called Ostrow. He found Janina without a pulse and even started filling out her death certificate. When she woke up, Janina asked for hot tea and pancakes.

"I was sure she was dead," said Dr. Wieslawa Czyz, a physician who examined her. "I'm stunned, I don't understand what happened. Her heart had stopped beating, she was no longer breathing."[1]

A surprising number of pastors, elders, deacons, and other church leaders I interact with seem to constantly be out of breath. Some are barely registering a pulse at all. While pushing bravely through to the next event on their calendar, these leaders often do not realize how weak their neglected souls have become.

Even more surprising is how often this depleted state is embraced as a normal way to live and serve. Since *soul* literally means breath, let me be bold enough to ask if you are breathing normally these days. If you are, there is vibrancy in your life. If not, then don't wait for a visit to the morgue to wake you up.

Philip Nation was the original content editor for this book. He is a pastor, author, and publisher, and has become one of my very best friends. In the early stages of discussing this book at a coffee shop with Philip, he made this hauntingly astute observation:

> Pastors can lose their sense of self in ministry.

If your ministry has been constantly draining the life out of you, perhaps you need to create a clearer separation of church and self. I have lost myself in ministry more than once over the last thirty-five years. There have been seasons when I did not have much of a life outside of my ministry, which is sad. Since our soul is our life, this chapter is a great opportunity to take stock of our lives, then bravely make bold, intentional changes that will help us get and stay emotionally healthy.

I want to challenge you to candidly check your emotional pulse by asking God whether your soul is awakened, downcast, and/or surrendered.

THE AWAKENED SOUL

Since *soul* is a synonym for the individual person, it is commonly and accurately translated as *life*—referring to your life right now, not the after-life. Christian souls do not need to be resaved, but they do sometimes need to be reawakened.

We all aspire to be spiritually and emotionally awake. The good news is that it is within our grasp to have a resilient, awakened soul that is fully alive. If your soul is sleepy and lethargic, you can join me in this simple, timeless prayer: "Wake up, my soul!" (Ps. 57:8).

Awakened souls learn to arrange their external lives to keep pace with their interior lives—not the other way around. Disciplined leaders have learned the fine art of prioritizing their schedules instead of rationalizing them. Growing as a leader will mean learning how to do this prioritization.

Healthy pastors will lead healthy churches and ministries because they have learned to lead themselves first. There are three basic disciplines that have helped keep my soul awake for thirty-five years of pastoral ministry.

1. Worship Daily

I genuinely desire to love God with all my soul, but this is a day-to-day discipline. There is no getting around the fact that our schedules accurately reflect our priorities because schedules don't lie or exaggerate. Since our aim is to love God with all our soul, our *first love* must have first place in our daily schedules.

The fact that the God of all creation wants to personally restore my soul each day is beyond amazing! Look at how God communicates this to us:

> "Come to me, all of you who are weary and burdened, and I will give you rest . . . for your souls." (Matt. 11:28–29)

Our walk with God needs to be consistent enough to find spiritual rest. Jesus invites us into his presence whether we are weary or not.

> "Remain in me, and I in you. Just as a branch is unable to produce fruit by itself unless it remains on the vine, neither can you unless you remain in me. I am the vine; you are the branches. The one who remains in me and I in him produces much fruit." (John 15:4–5)

The very first thing I changed after the "face mask moment" with God that I mentioned in the first chapter, was to consistently schedule a daily time with him. I live by my calendar, so when I looked at my overcrowded calendar fourteen years ago, I became convicted by how I had let my relationship with God dangerously erode. At that time, I was meeting a friend at the gym two or three mornings a week. I usually had one or two breakfast meetings each week on top of that.

Although I was pastoring a large church at the time, I had unintentionally squeezed Jesus out of the best part of my calendar. As John Ortberg says, "A paradox of the soul is that it is incapable of satisfying itself, but it is also incapable of living without satisfaction. You were made for soul-satisfaction, but you will only ever find it in God."[2]

I desperately needed to start my day with God, so I took "first" literally by immediately putting an end to all my morning meetings. That is still my practice today.

> As the deer pants for streams of water, so my
> soul pants for you, my God. (Ps. 42:1 NIV)

I assume that you regularly read or study the Bible, but how long has it been since you *really* enjoyed it? When was the last time your soul was strengthened and refreshed by the life-giving presence and Word of God?

Is your vision to grow your ministry more ambitious than your vision to grow your soul?

> The law of the LORD is perfect, reviving the
> soul. (Ps. 19:7 ESV)

2. Sabbath Weekly

Sabbath simply means "stop." It is number four on God's top ten list of commandments. Pastors and church leaders play fast and loose with their obedience when they work all week without stopping. Who are we fooling when we minister all day on

Sunday and call it a Sabbath? We disciple our people by modeling how to consistently obey God's command.

The Sabbath is not only a command, but also a gift that applies to all believers . . . including ministers. Ministry is often emotionally energizing but can also be emotionally draining when the weight of all our responsibilities gets too heavy.

One honest pastor wrote, "I was ready to quit if I didn't collapse first. I remember getting a plaque from some organization for being one of the ten fastest growing churches in the city (Minneapolis). But inside we were a mess. My personal life was a mess, because at the time I didn't believe you could lead a church and have a quality personal life. I thought the two were mutually exclusive. Our key staff were stressed and exhausted. A couple of us took the plaque into the woods, put it on a tree, and shot it full of holes with a rifle. We hated what it stood for. We felt like this bigness was killing us."[3]

You have likely felt like that staff team. Was it the crowded church calendar that emotionally exhausted you? Maybe it was a set of prickly members who drained you. Maybe there are some deacons reading this who have assumed temporary responsibilities between pastors. Maybe you are an elder who has had to discipline a church employee or member.

When ministry gets tough, you just want some relief.

Emotionally resilient leaders learn to come off the front lines of ministry between tough seasons of service. They have a life and identity outside of the church that keeps their pulse strong. I was coaching some pastors recently in Kentucky about the need to have a life outside of ministry when one of them flatly said, "I have a kayak I've not used in two years. I need to change that." Other pastors quickly chimed in, "I used to go hunting . . . I used to play golf . . . I used to garden" (that last dude lost me).

King David's soul was restored beside green pastures and still waters. Where does your soul recharge the fastest? I get recharged by bowhunting in the fall and competing in a tennis league in the spring. Is there a better time than now to enjoy the abundant life you preached about last Sunday? Self-care may seem selfish to those committed to serving others, but I assure you that an unhealthy pastor will do more harm than good.

I recently met with a weary soul who had pastored almost a decade without a vacation. Like many depleted pastors, he gave it all to the office. I am fearful that he will not finish strong—if at all.

There is a much better way to live.

There is a much better way to serve.

3. Discipleship Monthly

Pastors preach, teach, and lead members to see that Christianity is not a solo sport. We tell them not to try to grow alone, but do we really believe this? Nothing moves the discipleship needle more than pastors modeling it. Unfortunately, it is rare to find a pastor who is part of a group he does not lead.

As a leader, you need someone to lead you so that you can travel deeper in your faith and farther with your church family into God's mission. A discipleship group can be a conventional small group (S.S. class), a same-gender discipleship group, or a one-on-one mentoring relationship.

We just moved to Dallas a few months ago and have been diligently looking for a church family because we know that we need soul care as much as anyone—maybe more. Last Saturday Janet and I returned from leading a ministry marriage conference out of state, and we were exhausted. We were tired enough to consider skipping church, but instead we joined one. A few weeks later we joined a small group. We are not legalists, we are survivalists.

For the busy pastor who has no one investing in his soul, I want to challenge you to meet with someone every month—or a group—for the purpose of helping you grow. We need to be discipled just as much as those we are discipling.

Has your soul had time to catch up with your schedule lately? If your soul needs rest, make a change.

THE DOWNCAST SOUL

It is not realistic to expect our souls to always be in an awakened mode.

On our best days, our souls rejoice. On our worst days, our souls are *swallowed up in sorrow*, as was the case for Jesus in the garden of Gethsemane moments before his trials and crucifixion. We cannot love God and others with all our souls when our souls are sorrowful.

We saw in chapter 2 that the Greek term for soul is *psyche*, from which we get the English word *psychology*. Sigmund Freud said that his life's work had been devoted to understanding as fully as possible "the world of man's soul."[4] Even the secular-minded Freud saw the deep human need for a healthy soul.

There have been times in my life when I could really relate to Jeremiah, who was admittedly a tortured soul. Jeremiah said, "My soul has been deprived of peace; I have forgotten what happiness is" (Lam. 3:17 HCSB). For this weary soul, happiness was too often a distant memory.

Ministry leaders sometimes repress these emotions because they don't know what to do with them. Pastors prefer to be perky, so we usually fake it when our souls are sick. We like to be in charge, so we try to control our emotions, which seldom works for very long. I wonder if we do that because we have confused discouragement with sin or failure.

Would it surprise you that even Jesus sometimes experienced a downcast soul?

> "My soul is swallowed up in sorrow—to the point of death." (Mark 14:34 HCSB)

> "My soul is troubled." (John 12:27a)

The sorrows of life did not indicate sin or failure in our perfect Lord. He was simply in the middle of navigating the difficult course set before him.

Mary, the mother of Jesus, was told by Anna that a sword would someday pierce her soul (Luke 2:35). Instead of spiraling into depression, Mary's soul was strengthened through singing praises to God. In response to the word by Simeon, Mary replied,

> "My soul proclaims the greatness of the Lord,
> and my spirit has rejoiced in God my Savior."
> (Luke 1:46–47 HCSB)

Is your soul downcast about your children (like Hannah and Mary), about your ministry (like Jeremiah and Paul), or about your security (like David and Peter)?

Paul's downcast spirit was comforted through people like Titus: "When we came into Macedonia, we had no rest. Instead, we were troubled in every way: conflicts on the outside, fears within. But God, who comforts the downcast, comforted us by the arrival of Titus" (2 Cor. 7:5–6).

Remember that God's grace is enough and that our partners in the work of ministry can be agents of that grace. After pastoring three wonderful churches for twenty-seven years, I have had the privilege of serving pastors for the last nine years with GuideStone, Lifeway, Oklahoma Baptists, and the Care4Pastors Network. There are countless pastor advocates in ministries like these who are dedicated to helping you start well, serve well, and finish well—but you need to let them help you—especially in difficult seasons. In addition to my full-time job, I was pastoring a church during part of the pandemic, and it was one wild ride! But I was never alone.

I often tell young pastors and seminarians to expect and even embrace seasons of discouragement. The apostle Paul told the rookie Timothy to "Preach the word; be ready in season and out of season" (2 Tim. 4:2). I do not expect ministry leaders to enjoy tough seasons, but I also don't want them to be surprised by them because they are normal and usually temporary.

Intentional leaders will assess their seasons in real time, then make an ascent up Mount Perspective to see the bigger picture. Keep your eyes focused on the finish line instead of the inevitable obstacles that you must endure.

Pastors and leaders who move from church to church looking for the utopian congregation are in for a huge disappointment. Wherever you find people, you find problems. Resilient pastors learn how to create a healthy distance from those who are pastoral pariahs who seem to thrive on making our jobs harder. The primary reason people steal our joy is because we let them.

King David experienced several turbulent seasons in his life. He said in Psalm 42:5–6a:

> Why, my soul, are you so dejected? Why are you
> in such turmoil? . . . I am deeply depressed.

Although David often experienced the *dark night of the soul*, he always hung on to the hope that God was still firmly on his throne. God also spoke through Jonathan's voice to remind David of his bright future. If your season of discouragement sets in indefinitely, I would encourage you to talk to your family doctor or licensed counselor. Self-diagnosis is a waste of time, even if you are clinically trained, which most of us are not. If the fog of clinical depression has set in, the wisest thing you can do is walk through that fog with someone who knows where he or she is going.

THE SURRENDERED SOUL

Whether your soul is downcast, awakened, or somewhere in the middle, you should always be surrendered. The only way for our souls to stay anchored throughout life's storms is to abide with him daily.

Have you surrendered your soul/self completely to the Lord recently?

Don't answer that question too quickly. The stakes are too high for you to jump back into your ministry role with a partially surrendered soul. Soul surrender is a daily decision, not just an eternal one. As you read through this very familiar passage, read it slowly and keep in mind that all four times "life" is used, it is translating *psyche* (a.k.a. soul).

"If anyone wants to follow after me, let him deny himself, take up his cross, and follow me. For whoever wants to save his *life* will lose it, but whoever loses his *life* because of me and the gospel will save it. For what does it benefit someone to gain the whole world and yet lose his *life*? What can anyone give in exchange for his *life*?" (Mark 8:34–37, emphasis mine)

What part of your life on earth should be under the lordship of Jesus Christ? What does it mean to deny yourself? What would your life and ministry look like if you loved God with all your soul?

Take time right now to pray for a refreshed, restored, and revived life. Why not ask God to breathe afresh his Spirit into your soul/life this very minute?

CHAPTER 5

WITH ALL MY MIND

For the first two decades of pastoral ministry, my primary personal vision was to build a Great Commission church. That vision fueled two decades of uninterrupted church growth in three churches. That is, of course, if you only measure growth by baptisms, buildings, and budgets.

The problem was I was not personally growing at the same pace as my ministry. I was letting the work of God around me smother the work of God within me, the inevitable result being that my internal flame started to flicker, creating a ministry midlife crisis. Assuming I could build (or leap) tall buildings in a single bound, I eventually realized that I was a man of flesh, not steel.

Turning the world upside-down was fun until my world was turned upside-down with a three-year season of clinical depression.

I suspect that every pastor goes through temporary seasons of burnout and discouragement. A 2019 study called Flourishing in Ministry asked 10,000 pastors about their well-being. Nearly 25 percent said they were suffering in a very difficult season of emotional burnout and physical health. An additional 25 percent said they were very close to joining that first group.[1]

Tough days are a given. We must be prepared to serve and preach *in and out of season*. However, my season of discouragement drew me into a stubborn mental fog that refused to lift. I felt trapped and became so concerned that I reached out to my doctor for help.

That was over a dozen years ago, and I praise the Lord for completely delivering me from that dark season of depression. Like cancer, there are many types of depression, and the worst thing we can do as ministers is to self-diagnose. My MD and licensed therapist were both members of my church, and God used them both to get this Humpty Dumpty back on the wall again!

As a graduate of three Southern Baptist schools, I was surprised at how unprepared I was to assess and address my own mental health, much less that of the church members I pastored. As a result, I learned the hard way that the health of the pastor is intrinsically connected to the health of the local church.

I once shared my depression testimony at a pastors' conference in West Virginia, and received this response from a pastor:

> "Mark, I am thankful for what you taught us at
> the pastors' conference. I felt greatly encouraged

> to enter counseling. I have done just that and, man, I am beginning to see God's love and grace for me more than ever."

When a West Coast pastor who was in a dark place also took my advice about seeking help through clinical Christian care, his wife and daughters sought me out at the Southern Baptist Convention to thank me! Their fresh testimony of his healing brought a tear to my eye and a smile to my face. To God be the glory!

Twenty-six percent of American adults experience a diagnosable mental disorder each year, according to the National Institute of Mental Health. It should be no surprise that this same percentile (26%) of U.S. Protestant pastors say they have personally struggled with some type of mental illness.[2]

Please don't hear me saying that I think that most pastors are depressed, but more than ever they are reaching out for help. I lead Pastoral Wellness initiatives at GuideStone Financial Resources, and GuideStone recently reported a 40 percent increase in mental health claims since the COVID-19 pandemic started (2019–21).[3]

Depression is complicated and sometimes dangerous, but it is a treatable condition, not a terminal one.

Pastors and other church leaders should be messengers of hope and healing for those who constantly struggle with their thoughts. When people limp into our churches, we need to make sure they understand that they do not have to walk alone through a mentally foggy valley. Jesus and his bride are eager to help you live an abundant and fruitful life. As the writer of Ecclesiastes taught, "Two are better than one because they have a good reward for their efforts" (Eccles. 4:9).

We all desire to love the Lord with all our minds, and in doing so we should be able to pay attention to our mental health.

A NEW PRIORITY

Mental health had to become a priority in my own life before it became a priority in my ministry. Once I was healthy again, the church I served regained a vitality it had not seen in years. I get chills when I think about the intrinsic connection between the overall well-being of a minister and the local church he or she is serving.

You don't have to look too hard in the Bible to see how important a healthy, transformed mind is. Although mental health is about as unpopular a topic as physical health, both are clearly called out in the Great Commandment as well as throughout the rest of the Bible.

> I urge you to present your *bodies* as a living sacrifice, holy and pleasing to God; this is your true worship. Do not be conformed to this age, but be transformed by the renewing of your *mind*, so that you may discern what is the good, pleasing, and perfect will of God. (Rom. 12:1–2, emphasis mine)

I know it would be much easier for us to stick to the more familiar topic of spiritual health and skip all those pesky passages about the mind and body—if only the Great Commandment gave us that option. However, there is no need to be intimidated by these subjects because you and I are called to be equippers not experts. No one expects us to have a comprehensive understanding of the human brain. But as stewards of God's Word, we need to have a basic understanding of what it means to be Christian leaders who love the Lord with all our minds.

You know well that Satan has plans for your life, but let's not forget that God has even bigger and better plans. Jesus told Peter, "Simon, Simon, look out. Satan has asked to sift you like wheat. But I have prayed for you that your faith may not fail" (Luke 22:31–32a). Jesus was preparing Peter for the inevitable warfare that was just around the corner, but he was not sowing seeds of fear in him. Although I do not believe it was God's will for Peter to fail, he obviously allowed Peter to go through the sifting and refining process so he could grow in both strength and humility.

He would need both later.

We know in retrospect that God had big plans for Peter, but we also know that God has important plans for your life and ministry. Do you believe that Jesus is interceding right now for your good and his glory? Jesus is not pacing nervously around the throne room of heaven wondering if you will lead and live well. No. He is actively interceding for your faithfulness and advocating for you when you fail.

Envision the kind of leader you could be a year from now if you intentionally and consistently loved God with all your mind. How would you change your thinking in the next twelve months if you consistently submitted your thoughts to the transformational work of the Lord Jesus Christ?

The choices here are crystal clear. Either passively allow yourself to be conformed to this age or have your mind transformed and renewed by Christ. This simple choice is presented to each of us every day, week, month, and year: *conform or be transformed.*

If you choose not to intentionally submit to this transformational sanctification process, you are by default choosing to *conform to this age.* If you choose to *be transformed by the renewing of your mind,* you are committing to a slow, disciplined process of sanctification, which ends only in heaven. A transformed mind goes through a gradual maturity metamorphosis that pays off both in this life and the next.

The battle for our brain is not easily or quickly won. Don't get discouraged by setbacks. They are inevitable. Strong, healthy pastors and leaders don't easily back down from fights. Instead, we prepare for them. We gear up for battle.

Paul wrote, "Finally, be strengthened by the Lord and by his vast strength. Put on the full armor of God so that you can stand against the schemes of the devil" (Eph. 6:10–11). The root of the word *conform* (*schema*) is the origin of our English word *scheme.* Do you realize that God is fully prepared for the predictable schemes of the devil? Many of these schemes manifest in the stresses of church leadership. Some manifest in our own stress about church leadership.

CHEERLEADERS WELCOME

I talk to pastors and ministry leaders every single day and can attest to the fact that they have one of the hardest jobs on the planet. A 2015 Lifeway Research Pastor Attrition Study of 1,500 pastors revealed some of pastors' most common concerns:

- 84 percent say they're on call 24 hours a day
- 80 percent expect conflict in their church
- 54 percent find the role of pastor frequently overwhelming
- 53 percent are often concerned about their family's financial security
- 48 percent often feel the demands of ministry are more than they can handle
- 21 percent say their church has unrealistic expectations of them[4]

The results of this survey remind us that those who are still serving on the front lines of ministry need encouragers to root them on. The race is not over yet. If you are a pastor, find some encouragers to gather around you.

> Now finish the work, so that your eager willing-
> ness to do it may be matched by your comple-
> tion of it. (2 Cor. 8:11 NIV)

RENEW BY REFOCUSING

A mentally healthy pastor needs to do more than dodge evil thoughts; we need to intentionally think godly thoughts. Paul wrote,

> Whatever is true, whatever is honorable, what-
> ever is just, whatever is pure, whatever is
> lovely, whatever is commendable—if there is
> any moral excellence and if there is anything
> praiseworthy—dwell [think] on these things.
> (Phil. 4:8)

Donna Seal is a licensed professional counselor who had the challenge of having me as both her pastor and patient during my season of clinical depression. In her practice and seminars, Donna has helped me and countless others to intentionally think God-honoring thoughts that are truthful, hopeful, and helpful.

FOCUS ON WHAT IS TRUTHFUL

Some of our thoughts are simply not true. When deceptive thoughts creep into our minds, they need to be replaced by God's Word, which is always truthful.

We love God with all our minds by consistently reading and meditating on biblical truth. As we are uploading biblical truth, we are simultaneously off-loading the untruths that have seeped into our minds subconsciously.

> We demolish arguments and every proud thing
> that is raised up against the knowledge of God,
> and we take every thought captive to obey
> Christ. (2 Cor. 10:4b–5)

We must stubbornly refuse to fall for the lies of the enemy. Otherwise, we will become entrapped by the immoral, self-absorbed, unbiblical thinking in our culture.

Lies that people—including pastors—often tell themselves are:

- I'm a failure.
- I don't matter.
- God could never forgive me for that.
- I'm not as important as other people.
- This sin is not really that bad.

It takes no effort to believe lies about ourselves, God, and others in general. Those lies become ways of thinking, then believing, and then living. We will live out what we believe, so it is vital for a healthy and productive Christian to consciously believe truth and reject lies.

It is often hard to recognize a lie because we have entertained the thought so often that it "feels" like the truth. However, our feelings are rarely a good indicator of truth.

Two questions to ask to determine if something is truthful are:

1. Does God's Word agree with me?
2. Would I tell another person that it is the truth of God's Word?

The truth will always agree with the Scriptures.

Getting mentally healthy may seem intimidating, but there is nothing mysterious or complicated about staying mentally healthy. I find it helpful to journal my thoughts and prayers after I read a chapter or two of Scripture devotionally. In fact, the ideas used in this book were birthed from my personal journaling.

Freedom is just on the other side of the bondage of lies. It is where Christ's good work takes hold of us and sends us out into his world on mission. Paul said it this way: "For freedom, Christ set us free. Stand firm, then, and don't submit again to a yoke of slavery" (Gal. 5:1). This passage brings to mind a resilient pastor who is either sick of his sin, or simply sick of being sick.

I pray that you will see yourself as a victorious child of God, not a helpless victim or slave. Countless thoughts go through our heads every day. Not all of them are true, so pray for discernment.

Some believers in the Roman church "exchanged the truth of God for a lie" (Rom. 1:25). The original context for this verse is sexual morality. We need clear thinking if we are to lead others through the cultural chaos. If our own minds are unclear about the truth, we will lead others into the same mess. Pastors must be intentional about pursuing purity in our private lives. We likely all have friends who have disqualified themselves from ministry because of sexual immorality. Pornography and adultery are false fantasies that never lead to lasting fulfillment. Nobody stays clean and close to the Lord by accident, which is why we must focus on what is truthful.

FOCUS ON WHAT IS HOPEFUL

Hopeful thinking is not the same as wishful thinking. Hopeful thoughts are true, but also hard. For instance, "I'm not doing okay (hard truth), *but* I can get better with God's help (hopeful truth)." Some thoughts are true but can be hard to take, especially when it stings.

Lifeway Research and Focus on the Family partnered in a robust mental illness study that found most pastors are reluctant to talk about mental health with their congregations (66%). Meanwhile, family members (65%) and those with mental illness (59%) want their church to talk openly about the topic.[5]

Pastors are often the first responders to mental health challenges in our church and community. We can make sure that individuals and families with mental health struggles are welcome in our churches. What better place to help people love

Jesus with all their minds than the local church? We no longer need to outsource all our members' mental health challenges to secular institutions, because we are the equipping and healing hands of Jesus.

Most of those who are reading this book are pastors, missionaries, or other ministry leaders. You are often serving God behind the scenes where things can sometimes get messy. When things get hard, you know that making things better means you will have to lead people from where they are to where they need to be without overly discouraging them.

Being hopeful means shooting straight *with* them, not *at* them.

God never leaves us without hope. Healthy, biblical thinking always involves hope. Sometimes life is very hard, so hopeful, biblical thinking is often both true and hard. For example: illness, finances, relationship struggles, natural disasters, the state of the economy, and death are all hard issues. We can't escape the truth of that. Trying to escape that hard truth leads us into denial. It is always important to stay in the truth even when it hurts or is hard. However, only thinking about what is hard can leave us in a place of despair.

It is why pastors also need this message of hope applied to our personal lives. We will all face hard times and dark days. The way that we do that in our thinking is to be honest about what is hard and add the word *but* . . . so that it moves from being hard to hopeful.

Examples:

> "I just got a cancer diagnosis, and I am scared. *but* . . . we will wisely work with the doctors and trust utterly in God's power."

> "My spouse died, and I am grieving. *But* . . . I have family and a church that loves and supports me."

> "We have strife in the church. *But* . . . I will lead with confidence that God's Spirit can lead people to repentance and restore unity in our congregation."

Adding a thought that gives hope doesn't automatically fix the situation, but it does anchor us in biblical truth that God rules and guides our lives. It guards us from spiraling down into negative self-pity.

The very first verse I memorized as a new believer in high school was John 16:33: "I have told you these things so that in me you may have peace. You will have suffering in this world. Be courageous! I have conquered the world." That verse has been a life-vest of hope for me several times over the years. With Jesus we can be both realistic and hopeful with our thoughts.

FOCUS ON WHAT IS HELPFUL

In addition to developing habits of thinking that are truthful and hopeful, we also need to be intentionally asking whether our thoughts are helpful. Helpful thinking is not about pretending something is good when it isn't or denying hard aspects of life. It is about recognizing thoughts that are both true and good. Without a disciplined mind, we tend to focus and dwell only on the negative.

My counselor friend Donna shared a great example of helpful thoughts regarding her daughter Emily:

> When Emily was pregnant with James Patrick, she immediately started having problems and had to have bed rest. That was frightening, and she knew it was not going to be easy. He was born one month early and was on life support. Nothing about that time was easy. She put up reminders all over her house of things in her life that were *true* and *good*. I found those lists in the bathroom, kitchen, laundry room, etc. This gave her a perspective that even though this was a hard time, it wasn't all hard. There were many things to be thankful for and to dwell on and think about.

Moses instructed parents to put copies of the first Great Commandment (Shema) all over their houses to remind the whole family to love the Lord, the true leader of their homes. He commanded, "Write them on the doorposts of your house and on your city gates" (Deut. 6:9).

Notice that even the city gates (our workplace) were to have this command as a helpful reminder of who was large and in charge. That is intentional thinking, parenting, and leadership. As a pastor, you need to ensure that God's authoritative Word is helping to inform your daily life.

I am convinced that apathy is our greatest enemy when our minds drift into dark places. Passivity gives the world's images and ideas unhindered access to our minds. Don't hear me saying that our minds will become focused on God by simply thinking happy thoughts. We are at war and have been given all the tools we need to push back against the darkness.

Loving God with all our minds is more than popular psychology; it is solid biblical theology. Paul said, "The mindset of the flesh is death, but the mindset of the Spirit is life and peace (Rom. 8:6). We need to set (an active work) our minds on the work of God. What he does in us and around us is, by far, the most helpful work we can meditate upon.

Don't Give Up!

Our minds are a battlefield. Land mines litter it from our fleshly desires rooted in ego and self-satisfaction. The world and our enemy will assault us with thoughts of grandeur and accusations of worthlessness. It is why you must focus your mind. Paul

David Tripp wrote, "No one is more influential in your life than you are, because no one talks to you more than you do."[6]

You and I cannot love the Lord with all our minds without the Holy Spirit's help. Right now, take the necessary time to submit your thinking to God. Ask Jesus to renew your mind so you can finish what God started in you.

> Let us run with endurance the race that lies before us, keeping our eyes on Jesus, the pioneer and perfecter of our faith. For the joy that lay before him, he endured the cross, despising the shame, and sat down at the right hand of the throne of God. For consider him who endured such hostility from sinners against himself, so that you won't grow weary and give up. (Heb. 12:1b–3)

If you suspect you are leading in a fog of depression, resist the temptation to self-diagnose or self-medicate. Instead, reach out to your doctor or a mental health professional for help. A safe place to start is the Southern Baptist Pastoral Prayer Line, run by Focus on the Family, where you can get a free and confidential consultation: 877-233-4455.

Mental resiliency is not limping across the finish line, it is accelerating through it. Self-care is not self-centered, it is strategic, so do whatever it takes to get and stay mentally healthy.

CHAPTER 6

WITH ALL MY STRENGTH

I enjoy traveling throughout the United States and abroad to serve pastors, missionaries, and seminarians. When I fly, I anticipate the possibility of a Transportation Security Administration (TSA) agent rifling through my bags during one of their random baggage inspections.

Even though this is annoying and can be somewhat embarrassing, I understand it is for the greater good. Plus, the TSA agent always leaves a courtesy card in the bag explaining why all my stuff is messed up. So far, I have resisted the temptation to reciprocate by randomly searching the TSA agents on duty.

This chapter may feel like I am going through all your private stuff. But I am an encourager, not an inspector, so know that whatever I write is with the intent to help you, not humiliate you regarding your physical health.

We cannot cherry-pick the parts of the Great Commandment that we like or feel most comfortable with, and loving God *with all of our strength* takes us into some sensitive areas of physical wellness. If we are striving to love God with all our hearts, souls, and minds, it naturally follows that we want to also love him with every bit of the *strength* we can muster.

Why, then, is it so much harder to talk about our physical health than it is our spiritual or mental health? Perhaps it is because our motives are not always clear. Do we take care of our bodies to look and feel good, or to honor God? Are these motives mutually exclusive? My objective is not to whip you into shape, because physical wellness is more than just physical fitness.

There are many admirable motivations for taking care of our temples, but here I will highlight my top five.

LOVE FOR MY LORD

> Therefore, brothers and sisters, in view of the mercies of God, I urge you to present your bodies as a living sacrifice, holy and pleasing to God; this is your true worship. (Rom. 12:1)

On January 8, 1956, Jim Elliot, a missionary to Ecuador, became a living sacrifice. The Amazonian Auca Indians he was trying to share the gospel with took his life, as well as four of his mission partners. Full surrender includes our bodies as well as our hearts, souls, and minds. Elliot's worshipful response to

God's mercy was to literally lay down his life on the altar of missions.

One of the great statements that Jim Elliot made about his life was about the beauty of sacrifice. Elliot famously wrote in his journal, "He is no fool who gives what he cannot keep to gain that which he cannot lose."[1]

I believe that the starting point for loving God with all our strength is putting our bodies on the altar of worship as Elliot did. Our living sacrifice is not to be confused with Jesus's bodily sacrifice, which was for our salvation. Our daily sacrifice is not for our salvation, but for our sanctification.

In Romans 12, the apostle Paul transitions readers from the theological to the personal and practical. Laying our bodies on the altar means that we are surrendering ourselves completely, and in some measure literally, to the Lord. Surrendering is a daily act that involves the whole self, physical body included.

Paul reminded the Corinthian church that the body is part of our covenant relationship with God. He wrote,

> Don't you know that your body is a temple of the Holy Spirit who is in you, whom you have from God? You are not your own, for you were bought at a price. So glorify God with your body. (1 Cor. 6:19–20)

Pastors who love God with all their strength will be standing daily on the altar of worship.

LOVE FOR MY WIFE

My marriage is another motivator to stay physically healthy. When I said "I do" to Janet three and a half decades ago, was I giving her my heart, my soul, my mind, or my body? I was giving her all four!

Because I surrendered the exclusive rights of my body to both Jesus and Janet, they are daily sources of motivation for me to take care of my body.

On our wedding day, I publicly vowed to Janet that I would love her to my dying breath. I realize that I won't be as physically healthy or handsome when I finish my vows as when I originally spoke them. That is okay, because our temples were designed to be temporary. Although I made no guarantees to her regarding my expiration date, it was assumed that I would not short-change her by accelerating my exit. If I grow ill and dependent on Janet in my later years, I am confident that she will love me *in sickness and in health*. Still, I have no intention of neglecting my body now only to make her or our children pay the bill later.

Paul points out the covenant aspect to our bodies when he wrote,

> A husband should fulfill his marital duty to his wife, and likewise a wife to her husband. A wife does not have the right over her own body, but her husband does. In the same way, a husband

does not have the right over his own body, but
his wife does. (1 Cor. 7:3–4)

The original context for 1 Corinthians 7 was sexual purity. I am confident that there is no possible way that I can cheat on Jesus or Janet and get away with it. These two covenants are equally irrevocable in my book, as well as his Book where spiritual adultery and marital adultery are not without great consequences.

Chuck Norris jokes are funny because of the reputation he gained as a tough actor and stuntman, along with his legitimate martial arts credentials. Although he is twenty-five years older than I, and three inches shorter, I have no aspirations of taking him on. In his book, *Against All Odds*, Norris writes, "People often ask me, 'How do you stay in such great shape?' Truth is I must work at it, just like anyone else. I get up each morning and work out physically; Gena and I take time each day to read the Bible, pray, and exercise spiritually."[2]

There are no secrets or shortcuts to physical fitness. I can testify that exercising with your spouse amounts to a multitasking recipe for a healthy life and marriage. My love for Janet drives me to do everything I can to be a good steward of the body God gave to me.

LOVE FOR MY KIDS

I married a preacher's kid. My father-in-law, Gilbert Kendrick, recently turned ninety-two, and he still rides four-wheelers, fishes, hunts with a crossbow, and travels around the country with my mother-in-law. For the last few months, he has been helping my wife do construction projects at our house with large power tools. As I write this, Gilbert and Joyce are spending the summer in a camper in the Southern Rocky Mountains in New Mexico, where their other daughter lives.

Gilbert is a pastor who is finishing well. He and Joyce are ministry marathoners who have taken care of themselves all these years, and we are all reaping the benefits. They have also lived within their means financially, which has helped them to enjoy this season instead of enduring it. I've been taking notes, and so should you.

The Old Testament character Caleb is another strong finisher who inspires me. After forty-five years of waiting to possess the land, this eighty-five-year-old warrior was still healthy and enthusiastic about his life and calling. He not only outlived the other guys who spied out the Promised Land, he eagerly led the advance to possess it more than four decades later (Josh. 14).

From start to finish, Caleb led himself and others well.

Are you preparing today to finish strong later? Let's live in such a way that we can pastor well for all the days that God has called us to serve.

STRENGTH FOR MY MINISTRY

Ministry requires a lot of energy. When someone asks how they can pray for me, my most common request is for "stamina." I am currently juggling my full-time ministry to pastors with being an interim pastor, leaving very little margin for rest. Having done this in both Nashville and Tulsa, I can say that it has been simultaneously exhilarating and exhausting. I have a much greater respect for multivocational pastors!

Although I never grow tired of pastoring, I do sometimes grow tired from it. It is not always easy to identify the source of my ministry fatigue. Experts tell us that we cannot just compartmentalize our physical health from our spiritual, mental, and emotional health. For example, sometimes when I am physically exhausted, I find myself fighting off negative thoughts.

Rested, energetic leaders generally are more motivated, focused, and pleasant than their counterparts. Exhausted leaders tend to be unmotivated, unfocused, unreliable—and cranky. Some of those who are unintentional about their health make jokes about the disrepair of their bodies.

Energy shortcuts are abundantly available to help us sprint or limp through another stressful week. My go-to shortcuts usually include sugar and caffeine. If these shortcuts become staples, then my stamina is short-lived.

> I discipline my body and bring it under strict
> control, so that after preaching to others, I

> myself will not be disqualified. . . . Run in such
> a way to win the prize. (1 Cor. 9:27, 24)

As leaders, we need to be good managers of the gifts and ministry we've been given. Romans 12 not only talks about surrendering our bodies, but also speaks to serving the Lord and his church with our spiritual gifts. The grace that saved us is the same grace by which we serve (1 Pet. 4:10).

LOVE FOR MY SELF

Perhaps the most overlooked part of the Great Commandment is to love our neighbors *as ourselves.* It is understandably counterintuitive for ministers to talk about loving ourselves. It sounds like something from Dr. Phil, Dr. Oz, or even Dr. Seuss. But since our Great Physician is quoting these Great Commandments, we should listen carefully!

I'm not saying that to be healthy you must live up to Western beauty standards. Many fashion models and athletes are not normal or healthy according to BMI standards of health. Our culture is obsessed with physical beauty, which can lead you down a dangerous path to arrogance and insecurity. Physical fitness becomes an idol for us when our temples become the focus of worship instead of vessels for worship. Remember that the primary goal is to "glorify *God* with your body" (1 Cor. 6:20, emphasis mine).

Is it fair to say that if vanity is one extreme response to physical fitness, then apathy is its evil twin? Why choose between vanity and apathy? Reject them both!

Many of us grew up hearing, "bodily exercise profiteth little" (1 Tim. 4:8 KJV). That is the way Brits talked 400 years ago, but it misses the point entirely in the twenty-first-century English. The present tense of the verb "train" in the original Greek indicates that both spiritual and physical training should be a lifetime pursuit for Timothy—and us.

Another way of saying this is that physical training is good, but training for godliness is much better. "Training" (Gk: *gymnatize*) can also be translated "discipline." Exercise has several benefits to motivate you besides vanity: more energy, fewer food cravings, fewer depressive symptoms, improved memory.

One way to love yourself is to be a steward of physical health. God created your body so prepare yourself to use it for all your days for his purposes.

TOP THREE STRENGTH-SAPPERS

Sex, food, and work are all magnificent gifts from God! They are also some of the most common vices Christian leaders fight against. Pastors do not get an exemption from these temptations. Conversely, we incur a stricter judgment when we fail because of the public impact of our testimonies to the kingdom (James 3:1).

John points out three top blind spots for us:

> Do not love the world or the things in the
> world. If anyone loves the world, the love of
> the Father is not in him. For everything in the
> world—the *lust of the flesh*, the *lust of the eyes*,
> and the *pride in one's possessions*—is not from
> the Father, but is from the world. And the world
> with its lust is passing away, but the one who
> does the will of God remains forever. (1 John
> 2:15–17, emphasis mine)

If we are serious about loving God with all our strength,
we must prevent the lust of the flesh, the lust of the eyes, and
the pride of one's possessions from draining us of the strength
we need for serving God and others. Let's look at these three
strength-sappers.

The Lust of the Flesh

The *lust of the flesh* can describe many modern disorders
and addictions. Food and medicine often become blind spots for
Christian leaders because of their obvious benefits. However, too
much (or little) of a good thing can become a bad thing.

Prescription pills can be helpful or harmful, depending on
how you take them. We are just as susceptible to addiction as
the members in our church. "I drink a half a pint of vodka every

night to go to sleep," one pastor told me a few weeks ago. Pastors don't get a pass on trashing our temples.

The lust of the flesh describes an idolatrous lack of restraint for whatever the body wants, whenever the body wants it. Lust means "desires"—which is a neutral word. The gifts of God (food, sex, and the like) become a vice when misused. Sexual desires are normal, but without any rules or restraint, they will lead to dangerous immorality.

Our appetite for food is natural, unless we let our appetites become gods. Paul described worldly people this way: "Their god is their stomach; their glory is in their shame; and they are focused on earthly things" (Phil. 3:19). Leaders must guard against the temptations to allow our bodies to have mastery over our love for God.

The Centers for Disease Control and Prevention (CDC) says that 68 percent of adults are overweight or obese.[3] The National Institute of Health defines *overweight* as a waist circumference greater than or equal to forty inches for men or thirty-five inches for women.[4] More than a vanity issue, our physical health is an issue of risk about the longevity of our leadership. Loving God with all our strength not only determines how we will finish someday, but also how we will model discipline today.

Most people try to lose weight through exercise but fail because they don't change their diet. A good exercise plan will not even come close to accommodating for a poor eating plan. Restaurants and grocery stores are not necessarily going to be helpful for your dietary goals. We must intentionally choose to read the labels and count the calories.

Janet and I are not into fad diets or popular training programs. My personal fitness plan is to do two cardio and two strength workouts a week. Sometimes I combine them when I don't have time for four separate workouts. Health authorities recommend that adults get at least two and a half hours a week of moderate physical activity (like walking) and two days of strength training.[5]

Some of you may be handicapped by a chronic illness, accident, or some other physical challenge, which would make my personal fitness goals too difficult. My health goals, as well as my eating and exercise plan are customized to fit my body, age, and temperament—as should yours. Discuss your goals with your doctor before beginning any exercise program, but take it as a serious issue of guarding against apathy in this Great Commandment area.

The Lust of the Eyes

On February 21, 2019, I was preaching to a group of North Carolina pastors at Ridgecrest Conference Center when I noticed someone on the back row awkwardly raising their hand to interrupt me. A news alert had just gone out that Billy Graham died at his Montreat, North Carolina, home at ninety-nine years of age. This was a surreal experience for several reasons: Graham was less than four miles away from us when he died; like them—he was a North Carolina pastor; and the topic I was preaching on was "Finishing Strong." Someday in heaven I hope to thank Billy Graham for finishing my Ridgecrest sermon with his timely exit, as well as illustrating it with his testimony of integrity.

Billy Graham was a bold global evangelist who revealed his greatest fear in an interview with David Frost: "That I'll do something or say something that will bring some disrepute on the gospel of Christ before I go. And I want the Lord to remove me before I say something or do something that would embarrass God."[6]

Pastors and leaders need to pray and plan for each other's purity. We must bravely talk about the challenges that face us head-on every day of the week, not just on Sundays. That means we are willing to talk about our lives and help each other fight and win life's hardest lust battles.

Paul wrote in Romans,

> For we know that our old self was crucified with Him in order that sin's dominion over the body may be abolished, so that we may no longer be enslaved to sin. . . . Therefore do not let sin reign in your mortal body, so that you obey its desires. And do not offer any parts of it to sin as weapons for unrighteousness. But as those who are alive from the dead, offer yourselves to God, and all the parts of yourselves to God as weapons for righteousness. (Rom. 6:6, 12–13 HCSB)

Christians have chosen sides in an invisible spiritual war. Although our eternal victory has been secured in Jesus's resurrection, our daily battle against sin and Satan continues here in our earthly bodies.

If you are struggling with sexual temptation, do not be discouraged! You do not have to stay the way you are, and you do not have to fight those battles alone. Find someone in addition to your spouse to help you get and stay morally pure. You are not doomed to failure, "for sin will not rule over you" (Rom. 6:14).

The Pride of Possessions

Loving God with all our strength has several implications for our church. Pastors are often hardwired to work hard, which is good! I believe our identities are divinely designed to be intrinsically connected to our vocations. We should take a healthy interest in our work, but there is an idolatrous line we can easily cross when our ambitions become our addictions.

As pastors, we can develop jealousy for others' possessions. These possessions can be the wealth of a local businessperson, or the growth of a church that another pastor is experiencing. Our "success" is not always measured by the stuff you can touch and record on a report. We need to have lives that are filled with love for God and love for others.

Many ministry leaders are convinced that excessive stress is the unavoidable price of success. Being on call 24-7 is seen as a survival strategy for people intent on climbing the corporate or ministry ladder. Driven pastors feel compelled to answer every call, text, email, and social media interaction as soon as they get them. The toxic effect of being on call all the time eventually will wear you down physically, emotionally, mentally, and spiritually.

Others have found that the price of success often offsets its perks, so they work hard to avoid the work trap altogether. It should be said that not all ministry stress is toxic. Stress can also be a good thing when it serves to motivate us to meet a deadline or protect a loved one. When stress becomes the norm instead of the exception, it contributes to high blood pressure, heart disease, obesity, diabetes, depression, cardiac arrest, insomnia, and many other health issues. The average U.S. worker takes a week less of vacation now than in 2000, and 55 percent of workers decline to use all the paid time off their jobs offer.[7] Stressed-out pastors are usually sleepless pastors because stress is the most common cause of insomnia.[8]

I hope this has been more than merely a pep-talk about time management. This has also been about life management.

RESPONSE

If you want to get your life back, you need to answer these important questions:

- Is your ministry bringing glory to yourself or to God?

- Are you willing to make changes today that
  will help you finish well later?

What one thing can you do this month to honor God with
your body? Share that goal with someone who loves you and
might also need encouragement in this area of their life.

CHAPTER 7

ASSESS AND APPLY

Let's wrap up the first section of this book by moving from assessment mode to application mode.

Since loving God with 100 percent of our heart, soul, mind, and strength is what he desires most from us, then it should be no surprise that anything less disappoints him. Actually, "disappoints" understates the reality of it. A tepid response to God's love somehow makes God sick. When a first-century church demonstrated a lukewarm love for God, Jesus said, "Because you are lukewarm, and neither hot nor cold, I am going to vomit you out of my mouth" (Rev. 3:16).

How we love God is obviously very important to him!

His relationship expectations are the same for us today. Jesus not only wants to be first in our lives and churches, he demands it.

It is important to understand that this famously graphic rebuke to the church in Laodicea was motivated by a white-hot covenant love. It is not normally effective to demand love from someone, but Jesus's rebuke was a call to repentance and restoration for this specific church.

The letter to the Laodiceans ended with this encouragement:

> "As many as I love, I rebuke and discipline. So
> be zealous and repent. See! I stand at the door
> and knock. If anyone hears my voice and opens
> the door, I will come in to him and eat with
> him, and he with me." (Rev. 3:19–20)

See the dramatic contrast between Jesus vomiting them out of his mouth and having dinner with them? That contrast reminds us how important it is to have an accurate assessment of our spiritual health.

The Laodicean Christians lived in one of the most lucrative cities in Asia, but they had grossly underestimated their spiritual poverty, as well as their spiritual maturity. God described them in this way: "For you say, 'I'm rich; I have become wealthy and need nothing,' and you don't realize that you are wretched, pitiful, poor, blind, and naked" (Rev. 3:17).

At this point in the book, I should warn you that self-assessments can often be misleading, especially for pastors. Sometimes we are a tribe of unrealistic optimists. Researchers call this "the halo effect."[1] This is not intentional on our part, but seeing every glass as half full is not always accurate or helpful. Other ministry leaders struggle with pessimism because of the drama within our own hearts, homes, and congregations.

If you are serious about your own spiritual development, ask someone who is not impressed or intimidated by you for help. Every pastor needs to be pastored, so who is shepherding your soul today? If you already have someone in your life who will shoot straight with you without maiming you, then thank God for them!

THIRTY-DAY CHALLENGE

I want you to consider making a few practical changes for the next thirty days, that will help your love for the Lord keep growing. The Shema is an invitation for us to go all-in with our love for God. Each of these four components of the Great Commandment gives you an opportunity to make a tangible thirty-day commitment.

I will love Jesus with all of my heart.

Jesus is not knocking on the hearts of unbelievers in the Revelation 3 passage. He was clearly calling that church to repentance and restoration. Leaders who want to have real revival in their church must start by having real repentance in their heart. It must start at this deep place in our lives:

> "Love the LORD your God with all your heart. . . . These words that I am giving you today are to be in your heart." (Deut. 6:5–6)

Turn the following verses into prayers and allow God to reclaim his rightful role as the Lord and love of your life, then write down your thirty-day commitment.

> Give me an undivided heart, that I may fear your name. I will praise you, Lord my God, with all my heart. (Ps. 86:11b–12a NIV)

> "I will put my teaching within them and write it on their hearts. I will be their God, and they will be my people." (Jer. 31:33b)

> "For this is the covenant that I will make with the house of Israel after those days, says the Lord: I will put my laws into their minds and write them on their hearts. I will be their God, and they will be my people." (Heb. 8:10)

Solomon said, "Let us test and examine our ways, and return to the LORD!" (Lam. 3:40 ESV). The Shema is asking if we are all-in, starting with our hearts. The "most important commandment" compels us to ask the most important question of our lives: Am I loving Jesus with *all* my heart?

In the next thirty days I will surrender my undivided heart by meeting with Jesus daily (write a time and place):

_____.

I will love Jesus with all my soul.

Does your interior life need some rearranging? While my heart is the eternal part of my life that is fully redeemed, my soul (life) is constantly in need of being restored, renewed, and refreshed.

Most of King David's psalms were lament songs that revealed the sadness in his soul, but he also allowed God to restore his soul in green pastures and beside still waters (Ps. 23:3). Where are the "green pastures" that restore your soul, and when did you last visit them?

My soul soars in oak trees overlooking green deer food plots with a bow hanging next to me. Much of this book was written in a tree stand somewhere in Tennessee, Arkansas, or Kansas. Janet's soul is refreshed on backpacking trips across mountain ranges. Is there something you love doing that you have been delaying?

Just today I got this email from a pastor friend: "I've been on vacation and just shut down. Best thing I've done for myself in a while!" Let me tell you what many pastors refuse to accept: the church will survive while you are on vacation.

Mary's soul experienced both rejoicing and sadness: rejoicing initially at the news of her pregnancy, "My soul proclaims the greatness of the Lord" (Luke 1:46 HCSB), and sadness at the news of her son's imminent death, that would "pierce" her soul (Luke 2:35). Having a troubled soul is not a sin. It's a sign of humanity.

Jesus promised rest for every soul that asks for his help: "Come to me, all of you who are weary and burdened, and I will give you rest . . . for your souls" (Matt. 11:28–29). When was the last time you revealed the current condition of your soul to the Lord or a friend?

In the next thirty days I will allow Jesus to restore and refresh my soul by (a person/event to help you recharge this month):

_____.

I will love Jesus with all my mind.

If you are struggling with consistently negative thoughts, you should consider talking to a pastor, doctor, or therapist about it. It takes an equal dose of faith and humility for a leader to ask for help. Socrates said it well:

"An unexamined life is not worth living."

Examining what you feed your mind is always time well spent. It is sometimes difficult to love the Lord with all our minds when we are exposed to so much useless media. What could you do to protect your mind from images and messages that lure you from your first love? "Be transformed by the renewing of your mind" (Rom. 12:2).

Inventory your thoughts this week to see which ones are truthful, helpful, or hopeful. Consider a media or social media fast and fill in the extra time with a classic book on your reading list.

In the next thirty days I will ask Jesus to renew my mind by (what can be added or removed for a month?):

_____.

I will love Jesus with all my strength.

Since our bodies are temples of the Holy Spirit (1 Cor. 6:19–20), doesn't it also make sense that we should take care of them? Presenting our bodies as a spiritual sacrifice is a personal act of loving worship (Rom. 12:1)—so take a few minutes to assess the stewardship of your body.

As pastors, we need to look at our behavior patterns and ask if they match our spiritual priorities. Food, alcohol, drugs, and sexual lust tempt us. We all know that ministry is exhausting, but what can you do to walk away from the snares to our bodies?

In the next thirty days I will honor God with my body by (specific, realistic health goals):

_____.

MY PERSONAL GOALS

To help you get your mind around this thirty-day challenge, I want to share my four Great Commandment goals for this year (not month):

1. **Spiritual health goals** (*heart*): Read through a three-year Bible plan. Journal at least once a week. Memorize Ephesians 3:17–21.
2. **Emotional health goals** (*soul*): Have a daily conversational connection with my wife and take her out on a date at least twice a month. Connect weekly with my children and mother (phone or in person). Go on a monthly outing with friends.
3. **Mental health goals** (*mind*): Read two books a month, one of which is a classic. Speak twice a month with my mentor and my accountability partner. Engage in quarterly social media fasts.

4. **Physical health goals** (*strength*): Have two cardio and two strength workouts a week lasting at least thirty minutes each. Sustain a maximum weight of X pounds (X = none of your business!).

CHAPTER 8

WHO IS MY NEIGHBOR?

The fact that you have read all the way to this second section of the book suggests you are someone who finishes what you start. It also suggests that you are serious about both the Great Commandments and the Great Commission, which as you well know are intrinsically connected.

So far, we have focused on the first great commandment to love God. This second section of the book will focus on the second great commandment: to love our neighbors.

> "The second [command] is, Love your neighbor as yourself." (Mark 12:31)

I find it interesting that although the curious scribe only asked Jesus for the top commandment, Jesus answered a question the scribe didn't ask by adding this second and completely different command. Jesus was revealing the other side of the great commandment coin the scribe was looking for.

Both of these commands were initially introduced separately by Moses 1,500 years before Jesus combined them. The first command to *love God* was originally introduced in Deuteronomy 6 as Moses prepared to hand the leadership of the Hebrews over to Joshua.

The second command to *love your neighbor* was also introduced by Moses, but in a different part of the Torah—Leviticus 19. As far as scholars can tell, no rabbi or teacher before Jesus had combined Leviticus 19:18 and Deuteronomy 6:5. This has become a brilliant nutshell of the whole Bible, from which every verse hinges. Jesus effectively condensed Scripture into a dual statement the size of a company tagline:

> Love God . . . love your neighbor.

The bottom line is that God loved us first, then gave us the ability to love him as well as our neighbors. Without our love for God, our ability to love our neighbors would be limited by our humanity.

Great Commandment love is the glue that binds every page of Scripture to its Author.

It is essential to not get the Great Commandments out of their intended order. Both have weight, but not the same weight. One Bible mistranslation says, "The second [command] is equally important" (Mark 12:31 NLT). The second commandment is very important; however, without the first commandment, loving our neighbor amounts to little more than humanism.

These top two commands became the gold standard for Jesus's first-century apostles and followers (Matt. 22:37–38; Mark 12:30; Luke 10:27; John 13:34–35; Rom. 13:8–10; Gal. 5:14; James 2:8–11; and 1 John 4:19–20). They are not only a succinct summary of Scripture but are also the fulfillment of it according to the apostle Paul. In writing to the church in Rome, he stated,

> The commandments, "Do not commit adultery; do not murder; do not steal; do not covet;" and any other commandment, are summed up by this commandment: "Love your neighbor as yourself." Love does no wrong to a neighbor. Love, therefore, is the fulfillment of the law. (Rom. 13:9–10)

At my core, I'm a pragmatist, not a theorist. I hope that you walk away from this book doing more than nodding your head in agreement. I want to inspire you to truly love your neighbors out of the overflow of your love for your Father.

THE GOOD SAMARITAN

If you are not sure who your "neighbor" is, you are in good company. According to Luke's version of the Great Commandment conversation, that bright scribe didn't know either. When he asked Jesus, "Who is my neighbor?" (Luke 10:29), Jesus's answer came in the form of perhaps the most well-known parables in the Bible about the Good Samaritan.

Since this very familiar story is Jesus's commentary on the second great commandment, I think it would be worth your time to read it with fresh eyes and an open heart.

> Jesus took up the question and said, "A man was going down from Jerusalem to Jericho and fell into the hands of robbers. They stripped him, beat him up, and fled, leaving him half dead. A priest happened to be going down that road. When he saw him, he passed by on the other side. In the same way, a Levite, when he arrived at the place and saw him, passed by on the other side. But a Samaritan on his journey came up to him, and when he saw the man, he had compassion. He went over to him and bandaged his wounds, pouring on olive oil and wine. Then he put him on his own animal, brought him to an inn, and took care of him. The next day he took out two denarii, gave them to the innkeeper, and said, 'Take care of him. When I come back I'll reimburse you for whatever extra you spend.'
>
> "Which of these three do you think proved to be a neighbor to the man who fell into the hands of the robbers?"

"The one who showed mercy to him," he said.

Then Jesus told him, "Go and do the same." (Luke 10:30–37)

Jesus broadens our Western definition of *neighbor* to include more than the person who lives within our walking distance. He teaches that a neighbor is anyone in need of our help. Some of our neediest neighbors live across the street, while significantly more live across the globe.

The Good Samaritan has become an unofficial symbol of unselfish, humanitarian service. Good Samaritan awards are commonly given out to exemplary volunteers, generous donors, and heroic citizens. We even have a Good Samaritan Law that provides legal protection from liability for those who assist others in need.

My home church of Green Acres Baptist Church in Tyler, Texas, sponsors a Good Samaritan Outreach Center, which is an appropriate namesake. The fictional character in Christ's parable has attained an almost superhero-like legacy.

For those who follow Christ, the story of the Good Samaritan was meant to do more than inspire us toward unselfish altruism. The Great Commandment this parable illustrates is the root of our Great Commission missionary manifesto. Jesus's simple parable blows up our conventional definition of *neighbor*, along with our responsibility for their well-being.

THE ZEROES

To the first-century Jew, the idea of a "Good Samaritan" was ludicrous. The phrase was an oxymoron to them. It was like you or me saying, *jumbo shrimp, found missing, or deafening silence.*

Samaria was in the middle of the country and became a region for cultural pluralism. Conservative Hebrews (Jews) considered Samaritans to be ethnic and religious half-breeds: part Jewish (Hebrew; native Israeli) and part Assyrian (ethnic Iraqi). Their degrees and pedigrees were frowned upon by the highbrow religious establishment in Jerusalem. Five centuries earlier, Ezra and Nehemiah's nemesis was another infamously obnoxious Samaritan named Sanballat.

Equal part attorney and theologian, the inquisitive scribe was an expert in both the civil and religious law, which were virtually inseparable in that culture. Like most of us in ministry, he would have identified with the priest and the Levite in Jesus's parable, as they were all occupying different places on the same elite Hebrew social ladder. They would have also held in common their hatred for Samaritans.

The setting for the Good Samaritan was the Jericho Road, which was notoriously steep and dangerous. Dropping 3,300 feet from Jerusalem to Jericho (17 miles), it provided the perfect backdrop for an ambush. This would have made it more interesting and believable.

Also believable was the apathy of the priest and Levite who walked past their half-breed neighbor without so much as a glance. They were in a big hurry to get to Jerusalem to fulfill their rotation at the temple. They had no time for needy neighbors, especially ones they disliked.

To Jewish leaders in Jesus's day, Samaritans were social zeroes.

THE HERO

When Jesus, an uncredentialed rabbi, made a Samaritan the hero of his parable, the cringe factor of the crowd went through the roof! Instead of seeing Samaritans or Gentiles as their neighbors, they only saw undesirables and enemies. It seems that the first-century occupants of Israel had just as much trouble living with their neighbors as their ancestors still do today in modern-day Israel.

The primary target of this parable today would be modern-day church leaders like us. Both pastors and lay leaders should see ourselves as potential "zeroes" in this parable. We were the target of Jesus's biting story. Those who serve on the front lines of ministry often find it difficult to find unsaved friends outside of our churches. Yet a healthy and focused pastor will learn to love and connect with the lost.

I've never met a Great Commandment pastor who was not also a Great Commission pastor, but the converse is not always the case.

If we love Jesus, we will love those he loves. This parable is meant to remind us that every person is an image-bearer who is the object of God's love. It helps us to understand how to love our neighbors and even our enemies on both an emotional and practical level. By positioning the Samaritan as the hero of the story, Jesus showed a new way to see how to love one's neighbor.

GUT-LEVEL LOVE

The Good Samaritan *had compassion* on this stranger, then Jesus told us to do the same in Luke 10:37. The Greek word for *compassion* is the same word used to describe what the father felt in the parable of the Prodigal Son. This Greek word gives the idea of someone's insides churning—a gut-level love.

Compassion is an internal fire that compels us to external action. It evokes tears as we get drawn into other people's pain. It allows others' problems to become our problems. Compassion will grow with time when its source is the person of the Holy Spirit who lives in us.

Loving our neighbor compassionately does not automatically mean that we love God. Many non-believers are genuinely compassionate. But if we love God completely as the first commandment requires, then a genuine second commandment love for our neighbor will naturally flow from it.

The apostle John reminds us that sometimes the neighbors we are called to love are our spiritual siblings. He said,

> We love because he first loved us. If anyone says, "I love God," and yet hates his brother or sister,

he is a liar. For the person who does not love his brother or sister whom he has seen cannot love God whom he has not seen. And we have this command from him: The one who loves God must also love his brother and sister. (1 John 4:19–21)

Love compels us to love our neighbors—near and far. If our love does not reach across the globe, our love may not be coming from the heart of God. Evidence that our love for God is growing is that our love for the least, the last, and the lost is growing at a similar pace.

STREET-LEVEL LOVE

That Good Samaritan gave his neighbor first aid, then a ride, and a room. Did the victim ask the Samaritan for help? No. Was it expected? No. But as an example, Jesus told us to go and do likewise. John said it this way: "This is how we have come to know love: He laid down his life for us. We should also lay down our lives for our brothers and sisters" (1 John 3:16). A real love is an active love.

If your church or small group becomes aware of a need in your church or community, don't just throw money at the problem—get your hands dirty like the Samaritan did. If a discipleship group only studies the Bible and never serves the community, how different are they from the scribes and Pharisees?

When it is in your power, don't withhold good
from the one to whom it belongs. Don't say to
your neighbor, "Go away! Come back later. I'll
give it tomorrow"—when it is there with you.
(Prov. 3:27–28)

In New York City, a nineteen-year-old student had a seizure
and fell onto the tracks as a subway train was closing in. Fifty-
year-old Wesley Autrey heroically leapt onto the subway tracks to
cover him and said, "Don't move or you'll kill both of us."[1] Real
heroes don't stand by and watch their neighbors suffer or die.
They jump in and try to help.

Mother Teresa's team member was overwhelmed at the
Calcutta mission and said, "How do you possibly hope to feed all
the hungry people who come to your mission?" Her famous reply
was, "One mouth at a time."[2] I'll point you to John once again,
who wrote, "Little children, let us not love with word or speech,
but in action and in truth" (1 John 3:18).

OUR THREE NEIGHBORHOODS

I have categorized our *neighbors* into three relationship groups,
which I will call *neighborhoods*. Each neighborhood will be introduced based on its proximity and importance to you. Everyone in
your life is equally important to God, but hopefully not everyone
is equally important to you because, well, you're not God.

We all need a nudge to help us identify who our priorities are. God is not silent or subtle on who deserves our time and attention first. I want to encourage you to proceed bravely through these final chapters. Read them carefully and intentionally. Someone in your life may need a demotion or a promotion. Why? Your priorities may need some reordering.

OUR FAMILY NEIGHBORHOOD

Our family neighborhood includes our families, whether they're formed from biology or adoption, and our nuclear families, which of course, includes you. Church leaders are disqualified from leading our churches unless we can lead our own lives and families first (1 Tim. 3).

Even those of you who are not pastors need to understand the stakes for your pastor so that you can support God's vision for his life and ministry.

For that matter, deacons have the exact same expectations as pastors and elders, except for teaching. Healthy church leaders will lead healthy families and ministries, which is why pastoral wellness and resilience start at home.

OUR FRIENDSHIP NEIGHBORHOOD

Our friendship neighborhood includes our inner circle of relationships. This often includes church members and staff, as well as friends outside of our ministry.

In God's hierarchy of relationships, there is always pressure to be close to everyone so that we aren't guilty of favoritism. We will discuss something more dangerous than favoritism in chapter 10—isolation. Many ministry couples are walking through life and ministry alone, which is unhealthy, unnecessary, unbiblical, and unsustainable for those who hope to finish what God started.

OUR GLOBAL NEIGHBORHOOD

Our global neighborhood focuses on the unchurched, the unsaved, and the unloved, both near and far. A Great Commandment pastor will always be a Great Commission leader because he or she will love those whom Jesus loved—sinners. Since Jesus was *a friend of sinners*, we must follow him in this work.

As our love for God grows, an inevitable overflow of love for our neighbors will follow. Get ready to have your earthly relationships reexamined and perhaps reshuffled through the perfect lens of Scripture.

We need more Great Commission churches who are led by Great Commandment pastors. Are you ready to answer that call?

CHAPTER 9

MY FAMILY NEIGHBORHOOD

A few years ago, I took my son Brad to visit my cousin Perry, who is a successful television director in Hollywood, California. Perry purchased rooms for us in the Hollywood Hilton and treated us to fancy restaurants with valet parking. He took us to film debuts in famous Hollywood theaters and hooked us up with VIP passes to Disneyland. Those passes were worth every penny of my cousin's money! We did not have to wait in line for a single ride or show all day.

Brad and I loved that whole trip. Who doesn't like to be treated like a VIP?

When we returned home, nobody parked our car or brought us free food. Once again, we had to wait in lines and clean our rooms like the rest of the non-Hollywood elite.

Everyone likes to be treated like a VIP, but if everyone is a VIP, is anyone really a VIP?

God's Word is crystal clear about the priority of the minister's family—they are our VIPs (1 Tim. 3; Titus 1). In this chapter, we will navigate through the relationships within our family neighborhood as they relate to our ministry.

If you are living in a blended family setting, these biblical principles apply to your neighborhood just as much as mine. Consider anyone who shares your house, your name, or your budget as part of your family neighborhood—and love them like Jesus would—like VIPs.

QUEEN OF THE CASTLE

Weddings are designed to be a celebration of covenant martial love. They are a great starting point for you to declare that your spouse will be loved for your whole life. Weddings are also opportunities to clarify both a promotion (your spouse) and a demotion (everyone else).

I love how the Bible simplifies and clarifies my relationship priorities: Jesus is my first love, and Janet is my second. I do not have to overthink this divine pecking order. Our kids and parents are next in line, but neither will ever break into the top spots.

NEIGHBOR = nearest one

Janet is literally my nearest neighbor. I strive to make sure she knows there will be no competition from anyone else, including our own family and ministry.

Janet and I have the privilege of encouraging ministry couples and have spoken at approximately 100 ministry marriage events so far in the last eight years. At each event I ask this question:

> Have you heard of any other profession on the planet that requires someone to win both at work and home?

Scripture doesn't give ministers permission to be awesome at church and awful at home. We attempt to help them succeed at home and church because God requires that pastors lead both well (1 Tim. 3:4; Titus 1:6). Deacon couples *likewise* live with this expectation, although with less public scrutiny. A pastor and elder . . .

> must *manage* his own household competently and have his children under control with all dignity. (If anyone does not know how to *manage* his own household, how will he take care of God's church?) . . . Deacons are to be husbands of one wife, *managing* their children and their own households competently. (1 Tim. 3:4–5, 12, emphasis mine)

Sometimes the term *manage* is translated "lead," as is the case for the spiritual gift of leadership (Rom. 12:8).

The primary point of this little word study is to remind you that when you accepted the call to lead a ministry, you also accepted the responsibility to lead or manage your family and yourself (1 Tim. 4:16). Do not look around the room for someone more responsible than you for the health and resiliency of your life, family, and ministry. You won't fix a problem until you first see it and own it.

IS YOUR MARRIAGE GROWING?

Sadly, too many Christian marriages are already broken. Ministry divorce rates are no different than for the general population. For pastors, Great Commandment love must begin at home before we can have any credibility in our church or our community. The collateral damage of mismanaged homes is an issue for those who serve in any church leadership role—not just lead pastors.

Since your family is where your neighborhood begins, it follows that your spouse should always be the primary benefactor of the second commandment to love your neighbor.

So here is a big, fat, scary question I want to ask you: *Is your marriage growing right now?* If you are not sure, I want to encourage you to bravely ask your spouse at the appropriate time, then patiently listen. Then, pray for wisdom as to how to rearrange your priorities so that God's pecking order can be restored in your home.

In a roundabout way, we have already asked your spouse that question. In 2017, Lifeway Research asked 720 American pastors' spouses a few questions and here is what they found:

- 37% do not get the attention they need from their spouse because the church needs so much
- 35% of spouses often resent the demands of ministry on their family
- 44% believe the church expects the needs of their family to be secondary to the church
- 1:3 feel caught in a tug of war between church and family
- 55% agree it is difficult to balance church and family
- 31% of spouses plan quality time each week[1]

Don't be discouraged. In a 2015 Lifeway Pastors study, 94 percent of ministry wives said they are satisfied or extremely satisfied with their marriage, and nine out of ten said their husband being in ministry has positively affected their family.

Don't be delusional either. In that same research project, these predominately male pastors assessed their marriages much higher than their wives.

I wish I could say that I have never allowed my ministry to become my mistress, or that I do not still struggle with it today.

For the last eight years I have served full time as a pastor to pastors—currently with GuideStone Financial Resources, which is part of the Southern Baptist Convention. Although I am on the front lines of ministry every single day, there is no one pressuring me to pursue my spouse other than my weekly accountability partner, who I will introduce in the next chapter.

It takes intentionality and determination for Janet to receive the best of my love instead of what's left of my love. If I want my ministry marriage to grow, I must regularly reset my priorities. Our marriage has fortunately never stopped growing because of the amazing grace of both my King and my queen, but predictably some seasons have been better than others.

DEMOTIONS

Some new marriages struggle right out of the gate after the wedding. As newlyweds rightly assume their new place at the head of the relationship line, some parents and siblings go through withdrawals.

Mothers often feel it more than fathers because they have been so used to being at the front of their child's relationship line. The inevitable and biblical demotion is always healthy but is sometimes met with resistance, which creates unnecessary stress for the newlyweds.

I suspect Western weddings were originally planned with this demotion in mind. Weddings seem to be sort of a boot camp for mothers. Think about it—who gets to walk the bride down the aisle and dance with her later? Not mom! She has to sit on the sidelines silently.

Dad even gets a speaking part—"Her mother and I."

Pastors, watch the look on the mothers' faces when the unity candles get blown out. I'm pretty sure both mothers flinch because they both just got simultaneously demoted!

Pastors also need to sometimes demote church members to protect their marriage. Certain members can steal huge chunks of our time and much of our emotional energy, but only if we let them. Well-meaning staff and lay leaders will interrupt family dinners and date nights with quasi urgent texts, but only if we let them.

According to Peter Scazzero, "If you want to lead out of your marriage, then you must make marriage—not leadership—your first ambition, your first passion, and your loudest gospel message."[2]

Nobody wants to blow up your marriage, so demote them lovingly and patiently. Return their messages the next day in such a way that will motivate them to follow your lead in their own relationships. Demotions and promotions can be fantastic discipleship opportunities!

PROMOTIONS

When Simon Peter wrote about marriage, he said, "Husbands, in the same way, live with your wives in an understanding way . . . so that your prayers will not be hindered" (1 Pet. 3:7). Rather than allowing the work of ministry to compete with your marriage, let it complement your marriage.

Janet and I have three simple marriage goals, which have served us well for three decades:

- Connect daily
- Date monthly
- Travel quarterly

The quality and consistency of those excursions have usually been dependent on our season of life. When we were parents of preschoolers, we were constantly broke and exhausted. This didn't keep us from dating or going on road trips. They just made both a lot harder, shorter, and cheaper.

A friend once confided in Janet that she and her husband were planning their first getaway without the kids in six years. All of their children can drive, so by their own admission, it was long overdue.

Sometimes pastors neglect their spouses because they are *churchaholics*. In all fairness, some ministers' wives neglect their husbands because they are momaholics and/or workaholics. I heard pastor Robby Gallaty say to a group of pastors,

> You can lose your ministry and still have your
> family, but if you lose your family, you lose
> both.

We must be intentional about growing our marriages if we want them to thrive. **Your ministry will never be stronger than your marriage.** Big, annual trips won't make up for an absence of consistent dating throughout the year. I've seen some people try to resuscitate their marriage with fancy gifts, trips, and ninth inning promises to change. If you stop dating when you have kids, you may eventually have a marriage that is as empty as your nest. In marriage, you are either dating or you are drifting.

If it seems like I am picking on the guys, you are right. Men are called by God to be the leaders of our homes. If there is a problem in your family, you are more responsible than anyone else. Own it and work hard to become the godly husband and father you have been called to be. Just remember to save some of the grace of God that you preach every week for yourself, because you will need it.

We preach the gospel more clearly by how we lead our homes than how we lead our churches.

More than a century ago pastor Charles Spurgeon challenged the students at his Pastor's College in London about marital health. He said, "We ought to be such husbands that every husband in the parish may safely be such as we are. Is it so? We ought to be the best of fathers. Alas! Some ministers, to my knowledge, are far from this, for as to their families, they have kept the vineyards of others, but their own vineyards they have not kept."[3]

THE NEIGHBORS DOWN THE HALL

If you have children living at home, they are your next nearest neighbors. They deserve to have priority in our lives, right behind their mother. Our nuclear family is our most important discipleship group, which is why it should be no surprise that they are the focus of the original Great Commandment passage.

In Moses's first application of the Shema in Deuteronomy 6, it says, "Repeat them to your children. Talk about them when you sit in your house and when you walk along the road, when you lie down and when you get up. Bind them as a sign on your hand and let them be a symbol on your forehead. Write them on the doorposts of your house and on your city gates" (vv. 7–9).

Discipleship can happen anywhere, but it should always start at home.

A tech-free dinner table is a great place to start discipling our children. We need our families conversing instead of media surfing. The American Academy of Pediatrics says that children spend an average of seven hours of screen time each day, while teens go at it for at least eight hours.

Next-level parenting looks like bedtime prayers and devotions when they are younger, and intentional conversations when they are older. Creating and personally practicing tech-free periods of time for your family will show them that you love them more than your ministry or hobby.

When our daughter Holly was very young, I could fake fatherhood pretty well. She didn't seem to mind when I literally fell asleep on the floor in the middle of a Barbie tea party. When she became a pre-teen, I reached out to my wife for wisdom on how I could stay connected to Holly as she matured. Janet's sage advice was, "Get into her world." Holly is our creative child, with a passion for music, baking, and art. Art was off the table for me, so I focused primarily on connecting to her through music (concerts) and food (restaurants). Last year, we revisited that season by attending a Toby Mac concert together at twenty-eight and fifty-six years of age.

Our children begin life as the center of our attention. Over time, we must prepare them for adulthood by helping them not be self-centered. But, as leaders in our homes, we cannot use ministry as an excuse to ignore our kids.

When U.S. Congressman Paul Ryan was asked to serve as Speaker of the House in 2015, he agreed under the condition that he would not travel as much as previous Speakers because he said, "I cannot and will not give up my family time."[4]

Three years later he decided not to run for reelection so that he could spend more time with his family—to avoid becoming a "weekend dad." Ryan said, "If I am here for one more term, my kids will only have ever known me as a weekend dad. I just can't let that happen. So I will be setting new priorities in my life."[5]

I personally think Paul Ryan was on an unhindered path to be the Republican Party presidential candidate when he bravely demoted the whole country in favor of his children.

As pastors, we must choose how we will lead and love our spouse and children. We must lead the way in modeling discipleship at home.

When Lifeway Research asked ministry spouses about their children, this is what they said:

- 1 out of 3 of spouses say their kids resent the demands of ministry.
- 1 out of 4 of spouses say their kids often don't want to go to church.
- 38% of spouses think their congregation expectations for their children are unreasonably high[6]

I've heard it said, "You will be a pastor to many members, but you will be the only father to your children." Pastors are not the only churchaholics out there. Ministry orphans and widows abound in the homes of missionaries, denominational leaders, deacons, elders, teachers, and ministry team leaders as well. Spend quality time with your family today instead of living later in the land of regrets. Take your vacations every year because your church can do without you, but your family cannot.

On a positive note, I am encouraged by a family-first trend that I have noticed among younger pastors and church leaders.

Perhaps they have learned from the mistakes of their predecessors or their own parents.

A good example of this is "Joe and Karen," who are serving as missionaries in rural south Asia. I had the privilege of being their pastor when they met in our college ministry in Arkansas. Soon after having their first child, they were faced with a difficult decision, which they explained in this letter.

> Over the past year and a half, we have called "Baytown" home. We have been by ourselves as the first and only foreigners to live in this town. In some ways, that has been amazing, and we wouldn't trade it for anything. In other ways, it has been the hardest year and a half of our lives. While we don't question the Lord's desires to move in hearts here, we also know he desires his children to be in community, which we have not truly had since we moved here. This month we will be moving to a city we call the "Windy City." What we hope the Windy City will represent for us is not just community and long term health, but also a very strategic placement to impact a broader swath of the unreached in the area through the university in that city. It will mean other foreign kids will be friends with our little one.

This wise missionary couple decided to make difficult, strategic changes that benefitted their family. Our children are not just part of our ministry, they are our ministry. Healthy Great Commission leaders will have healthy Great Commandment relationships, starting with their Savior, their spouse, and their children.

LOVING OUR PARENTS

Your season of life will determine who needs you most. Janet and I are empty nesters, and our parents need us more than our adult kids do right now. Paul wrote to his young mentee-pastor Timothy, "But if anyone does not provide for his own family, especially for his own household, he has denied the faith and is worse than an unbeliever" (1 Tim. 5:8).

About a week before my dad died last year, he finished reading an advanced copy of this book and blessed me with very encouraging feedback. My dad was a faithful deacon and Sunday school teacher for more than fifty years. He and Mom practiced Great Commandment love at home, church, and in their community. What a legacy I've been blessed to inherit!

My sister, Melissa, is married to a pastor, and they live close to my mother. The way Melissa and Pete Patterson have cared for our parents has been a clinic in what 1 Timothy 5:8 looks like. Janet's parents live close to us, and we are eager to show Great Commandment love to them as they live out their nineties.

LOVING OURSELVES

Perhaps the most awkward and overlooked Great Commandment relationship is the one found at the end of it: "Love your neighbor as yourself."

Some people don't need any encouragement in loving themselves, yet a healthy love for self is important. It is unnatural and unhealthy to neglect your God-given instincts of self-preservation. The key is to discern between self-centeredness and self-sacrifice. Nobody wins when we either exalt ourselves or neglect ourselves.

> Pay close attention to your life and your teach
> ing; persevere in these things, for in doing this
> you will save both yourself and your hearers.
> (1 Tim. 4:16)

"Pay close attention" (CSB) is a present, active, imperative verb, which suggests we will have to pay close attention to our lives as long as we have a pulse. Other translations say, "watch your life . . . closely" (NIV); "keep a close watch on yourself" (ESV).

This Greek verb literally means "to fix attention on; to hold upon." Those like me who struggle with attention deficit disorder know that the struggle to stay focused is real. The context to this important verse is a mentoring relationship between pastors—so please take this personally and seriously. Also, the stakes are very high, "for in doing this you will save both yourself and your hearers."

According to Paul's letter to the Ephesians, some of their church leaders left their souls unguarded, shipwrecked their faith, and sabotaged their ministry. So, it is no surprise that his last words to the Ephesian elders was, "Be on guard *for yourselves* and for all the flock of which the Holy Spirit has appointed you as overseers" (Acts 20:28, emphasis mine).

Self-care is not selfish, it is strategic.

In the relationship hierarchy, Jesus expects us to love God more than we love ourselves, and to love our neighbors *as* ourselves. Loving yourself is only at odds with loving God when we put ourselves in front of him. We live a life of self-denial in terms of our followership of the Lord.

Jesus said, "If anyone wants to follow after me, let him deny himself, take up his cross, and follow me. For whoever wants to save his life will lose it, but whoever loses his life because of me and the gospel will save it" (Mark 8:34–35).

Taking yourself off the throne of your life is a prerequisite for both salvation and ongoing sanctification. However, the death and denial of self is not to be confused with self-neglect or hatred, which is, paradoxically, an insult to our Creator.

The same can be said about loving ourselves to the point of selfishness with other people. Notice in this next verse the absence of self-neglect in genuine unselfishness:

> Do nothing out of rivalry or conceit, but in
> humility consider others as more important
> than yourselves. Everyone should look out not

only for his own interests, but also for the interests of others. (Phil. 2:3–4 HCSB)

Is God asking us to neglect our *own interests*? Paul suggests
that humility motivates us to put others in line ahead of us, not
take ourselves out of the line completely. Be careful not to over-
look that powerful little word—*also*.

The biggest daily challenge I face in being a Great
Commandment leader is overcommitment. I used to say "yes" to
almost every ministry opportunity that came my way for these
reasons:

- I love God and want to use the gifts he
  gave me.
- I love his bride and enjoy helping her leaders thrive.
- I need to be needed and thrive on
  appreciation.

That last one was difficult to write. I should have only godly
motives to blame for my ministry addiction. I've used the "God
card" more than a few times to justify the hole I've dug for
myself.

Most of you are familiar with the preflight mantra of flight
attendants, "Should the cabin lose air pressure, oxygen masks
will drop from the overhead area. Please place the mask over your
own mouth and nose before assisting others."

By the way, there are no secrets or shortcuts to self-care. Fads are for suckers. Yet self-care is awkward and counterintuitive for caregivers. We naturally want to help others before we help ourselves. But we are no good to others if we are passed out on the plane—or the pew. Self-care can either be self-centered or strategic, depending on our motives.

How and if you finish later will, in large part, be determined by how you care for your family and yourself today.

QUESTIONS FOR REFLECTION

1. Is there anyone who needs a demotion in your life right now?

2. What one thing can you do to become a better listener at home?

3. Name one specific way you can pursue your spouse this week.

4. Name two specific ways you can take care of yourself better.

5. If you are a pastor, who is pastoring you?

CHAPTER 10

MY FRIENDSHIP NEIGHBORHOOD

British explorer Henry Worsley died attempting to be the first person to cross the Antarctic unaided on January 24, 2016. CNN called it, "an epic charity mission inspired by polar explorer Sir Ernest Shackleton."[1] One hundred years after Shackleton's failed attempts to achieve the same goal, Worsley tragically died just thirty miles short of completing it himself.

When I read the story, I felt a strange sense of sadness for both of these brave British explorers who worked so hard, only to both fall just short of their goals.

My second thought was how stupid the goal was in the first place. Was crossing the Antarctic *unaided* even a sane goal for Worsley? Was it a brave adventure or a fool's errand for this fifty-five-year-old former British army officer to trek 913 miles for 71 days across the South Pole—*alone*?

> Pastors who attempt to do ministry alone are in
> grave danger of falling short of their finish line.

As the apostle Paul neared the finish line of his life and ministry, he serendipitously stated, "I have fought the good fight, I have finished the race, I have kept the faith" (2 Tim. 4:7). Paul traveled approximately 10,000 miles in his missionary journeys, but never alone. This is the key to finishing strong, friends. We know the names of the handful who abandoned Paul, but we also know the names of thirty-three he named at the end of Romans who helped him finish well.

Do you relate more to Henry Worsley or Paul of Tarsus?

I hope you don't see a strong ministry finish as an elusive goal reserved for elite leaders. Paul believed that a successful finish was the result of what Jesus did, not what he [Paul] did: "He who started a good work in you will carry it on to completion until the day of Christ Jesus" (Phil. 1:6).

My personal thirty-five-year ministry journey would have ended a long time ago had it not been for the countless encouragers who have believed in me when I wanted to quit. Some of you are reading this book and suspect that I am talking about you. I can remember all the Aarons and Hurs who have held up my arms when I grew weary. I can't thank them enough. The relationship groups I've described in this book have become guardrails for me against isolation, loneliness, and failure.

Pastor, I hope that you will make many friends in the ministry, but please do not stop there. Pursue friendships outside of ministry, which will lead to a richer life and a healthier ministry.

If you don't have a Barnabas in your life, you are missing out, or worse—burning out.

RIDE-OR-DIE FRIENDS

I have asked thousands of pastors in North America these two simple questions:

1. Outside of your family, who is your best friend"
2. When is the last time the two of you talked?

Until recently, my easy answer has been Paul Coleman and Craig Miller. I talked to both of them every other week for over thirty years. Since I couldn't have two best men, I asked Craig to stand in front of me to help perform the service while Paul stood next to me as my best man. For three decades these two have been my Aaron and Hur.

Paul Coleman has been my best friend and accountability partner since 1982. We became close in high school and were roommates in college. We even attended the same seminary and stood as best men in each other's weddings. We have never served on staff in the same state, but we have maintained a weekly call to check in on each other for our entire ministries. It was on one of those calls that he suggested the title of this book, *Start to Finish*. How cool is that? He has always been more creative than I, which is why it took him two minutes to come up with something I had been racking my brain over for weeks!

We have chosen to intentionally grow our friendship for the last forty years instead of leaving it to chance and letting it gradually fade like most friendships do.

Craig Miller and I became close friends in college. He took me on my first deer hunting trip, and I took him on his first mission trip. We took many other mission trips together, including the Baghdad trip mentioned in the introduction of this book. On June 10, 2016, we talked at length about the next mission trip we would go on together in Tanzania, where his international relief ministry, Thirst No More, was drilling water wells and planting churches. We were also planning to hunt while we were there, of course.

Two days after that call, Craig died in a freak accident on his farm.

I was undone.

The fact is, I have never lost anyone that close before or experienced that level of grief. My greatest consolation was that we had stayed in touch all the way up to the end. Hardly a week went by when we did not connect with and encourage each other.

I have lived and served together with Paul and Craig on the front lines of an invisible holy war, always with the knowledge that I never had to fight alone. These ride-or-die friendships are rare and will only grow if they are cultivated.

Who is helping you finish what God started? When is the last time you talked to them? The people you only hear from when you are winning are your fans, not your friends.

A HEALTHY FEAR OF FAILURE

My loyalty to Paul and Craig and a handful of other close friends is based on an unconventional mixture of love and fear. Within my first year of pastoral ministry, I watched televangelists Jimmy Swaggart and Jim Bakker fall in a very public way because of private moral failures.

Closer to home was the rise and fall of pastor Billy Weber from Prestonwood Baptist in Dallas. As a young pastor, I had stood in awe of Weber and other powerful speakers who were larger than life. Ironically, Weber's successor, Jack Graham, has led Prestonwood with integrity for thirty-four years, and we joined Prestonwood soon after moving to Dallas.

Within this same early season of my ministry, I watched two other pastors fail, both of whom I considered personal mentors and ministry heroes. Both walked away from their pulpits because of sexual misconduct.

At an impressionable twenty-two years of age and in my first pastorate, I became frozen in fear of failure. Having just started my ministry race, it was hard to conceive finishing well in four to five decades, especially since these prominent pastors could not even get halfway through.

I admit that some of my fear was fleshly. I knew my blind spots were not so dissimilar to any of those men. But I also embraced a healthy fear, which compelled me to ask Paul and Craig to stay close and hold me accountable for my personal growth and purity.

Janet and I both saved ourselves for marriage and have fairly uneventful testimonies for a deacon's kid (me) and preacher's kid (her). I wanted desperately to finish my marriage and ministry with the same integrity that I started with. Thankfully, God convicted me that a life of ministry would require more than a solo effort. I've been blessed to have Paul and Craig disciple and encourage me, but most of all I have the Holy Spirit to empower and protect me along the way.

So do you, friend, so be encouraged! And while you are at it, pray for an opportunity to encourage someone from the generation behind you as well as the generation in front of you. Most of us could use some age and ethnic diversity in our friendship neighborhood.

FRIENDSHIPS AT CHURCH?

Can pastors have friendships in the churches they serve in? When I became a pastor, the conventional wisdom among ministers was that a pastor should not become friends with church members. It was an understood assumption. It was talked about openly and, for the most part, went unchallenged.

At first, I bought into this line of reasoning. Part of me liked the us-and-them mentality because it made me feel superior. A larger part of me resented it because I wanted to be an intimate part of the faith family I was leading. Whether you are a pastor or a lay leader in your church, **I urge you not to confuse friendship with favoritism**. Otherwise, you are vulnerable to the isolation trap. Your church is more than your job, they are your family.

Matthew, Mark, and Luke give a very similar account of the Great Commandment conversation between Jesus and the scribe. However, the Gospel of John sums up the commands in his own unique way:

> "I give you a new command: Love one another. Just as I have loved you, you are also to love one another. By this everyone will know that you are my disciples, if you love one another." (John 13:34–35)

You may be wondering what is so new about this *new command*. Here, Jesus expands the application of the second Great Commandment to include loving our spiritual family. John surmises that our love for our sacred siblings is the ultimate proof whether our faith is genuine or fake:

> If we love one another, God remains in us and
> his love is made complete in us. . . . We love
> because he first loved us. If anyone says, "I love
> God," yet hates his brother or sister, he is a liar.
> For the person who does not love his brother or
> sister whom he has seen cannot love God whom
> he has not seen. And we have this command
> from him: The one who loves God must also
> love his brother and sister. (1 John 4:12b, 19–21)

Your church certainly needs you, but you need them just as much. If you don't already have a friend in your life, maybe you should look within your own church. Additionally, look beyond your church into the community where you live. Broaden your friendship neighborhood to include people who do not look like you, believe like you, or vote like you.

Is befriending church members and staff risky? Yes! I have a few scars to prove it, but I also remember the hollow pain of loneliness when I have pulled away from my church family. Our fellow staff members and church leaders are the closest people to us in the work of ministry. They are in the trenches with us. It is foolish to stiff-arm the ones who are blocking and tackling for you.

Pastoring pastors from coast to coast for Lifeway, GuideStone, and Care4Pastors has allowed me the opportunity to get feedback from those I would have otherwise never met.

A pastor named Bill gave a response to one of my Lifeway blog posts that gives us a glimpse into the typical reluctance pastors have when befriending their members:

> **Bill:** Remember that they [members] are the ones who sign your check; and since friendship requires vulnerability and transparency, a pastor should tread lightly there because friend or not, you're always going to be the "pastor."

> **Mark:** Thanks for reading and responding, Bill. You are right about treading lightly with church friendships. We do indeed have those layers of financial dependency and spiritual authority, but the same could be said of those under our roof at home. Whether we are loving our nuclear family or spiritual family, we usually have several complicated layers. We just need to make sure those layers are not excuses to neglect ourselves or them.

You must decide whether your church is just your job or also your extended family. If you are surrounded by strangers each Sunday, you have no one to blame but yourself. A good preacher speaks well, but a good pastor listens well. Friendships grow whenever we learn to do both well and in equal measure.

EVERY MINISTER NEEDS A MENTOR

Moses had Aaron; Elijah had Elisha; Zerubbabel had Haggai; Paul had Ananias and Barnabas; Timothy and Titus had Paul; and I have Tony plus a couple of retired pastors.

The origination of the term *mentor* came from a Greek novel. Before going away to fight the Trojan War, the fictional character Odysseus asked Mentor to raise his son as if he were his own flesh and blood. We need to have that level of discipleship investment in someone.

For three decades, I have made an intentional effort to have at least one mentor and a handful of mentees in my life. Each of these relationships has a reciprocal nature to it, which is consistent with the Barnabas-Paul-Timothy model passed down for two millennia.

I have noticed that younger pastors and leaders are generally eager to have mentors. This trend is extremely encouraging. I believe that the healthiest pastors are those who surround themselves with mentors.

MENTORING 101

Pastoral resilience is not realistic or sustainable without the help of other pastors. So why don't more pastors receive this kind of support from other pastors? The primary reason, in my opinion, is that we don't ask or know what to look for.

What does a Barnabas-type friendship look like? Here are six attributes that Barnabas modeled for a ministry mentorship.

A Barnabas will be supportive.

Every single pastor and ministry leader needs a Barnabas who will speak words of encouragement, and sometimes offer a rebuke, into their lives. When his nephew John Mark "wimped out" on his first mission trip, Paul wanted to permanently kick him off the team. Barnabas chose instead to mentor Mark, who got back on his feet and became a contributing author to the best-selling book in history. Mark would also become an invaluable partner to Peter, and yes, even Paul.

A Barnabas will be unselfish.

In Acts we read about the generosity of this church leader: "Barnabas . . . sold a field he owned, brought the money, and laid it at the apostles' feet" (Acts 4:36–37).

You have enough takers in your world. A Barnabas is the type of friend who will think of your needs as more important than his own (Phil. 2:3).

A Barnabas will be loyal.

When the Jerusalem church leaders sent Barnabas to Antioch to preach, he took along a risky new convert named Saul (a.k.a. Paul). Paul had a reputation for persecuting Christians before his conversion, and few assumed Paul was really a Christian. However, the apostles trusted Barnabas, and Barnabas trusted

Paul. Otherwise, Paul may not have gotten his first ministry opportunity (Acts 11:22–30).

A Barnabas will be mature.

When the church at Antioch began to grow exponentially through the conversion of Gentiles, the leaders in Jerusalem became a little nervous. They sent Barnabas to check it out: "For he was a good man, full of the Holy Spirit and of faith" (Acts 11:24).

We all need a confidant to share victories and defeats with— someone to talk us off the cliff of ministry suicide when we are on the verge of a tantrum.

A Barnabas will be humble.

Paul was a good writer and speaker, yet there was no evidence of Barnabas doing either. Most Christians are not called or gifted to take up the pen or microphone, so we may be tempted to assume that our gifts are inferior to those on stage.

Somewhere along the way, "Barnabas and Paul" became "Paul and Barnabas," a change that Dr. Luke subtly, but intentionally, makes in the book of Acts.

A Barnabas will be bold.

Barnabas was more than just a nice guy. He didn't back down from Paul when they had a sharp disagreement about John Mark (Acts 15:36–39). Followers of encouragement don't look casually beyond our weaknesses; they walk through those challenges with us.

Some lead best from the stage, while others, like Barnabas, lead best from the shadows. Barnabas is not credited with having written a word of the New Testament. But through his impact on the lives of the apostle Paul and John Mark and their subsequent influence on other writers, it is possible to say that Barnabas had a significant role in much of the New Testament. That would make him truly an "unsung hero" of the New Testament.

My primary mentor is Tony Weston, who watches over my life like a *big brother*, which is the nickname some of us who served on staff have given him. We served on staff together for nine years in Conway, Arkansas. When he left the church to start a marriage ministry, I was no longer his boss, so I asked him to be my formal mentor.

We chose to get intentionally closer rather than drift away gradually. Even though we do not currently live in the same state, I try to call him monthly and meet with him in person once or twice a year. If you are serious about pastoring all the way to the finish line, find a mentor who will coach you up. It helps if they have a few more birthdays than you and are the same gender.

Pastors need more sons of encouragement who are committed to helping other pastors succeed. Who are you encouraging, and who is encouraging you?

CHAPTER 11

OUR GLOBAL NEIGHBORHOOD

Not long ago I met with a young ex-convict I'll call Steve. The 90-minute meeting at a local coffee shop was not a meeting by chance or one of convenience. At the request of his family, I have been intentionally mentoring Steve for over a year. Because of the nature of his crime, we are limited to only a handful of meeting location options. But I really don't mind the inconvenience because I care about him. After all, Steve is my neighbor.

Tomorrow I will meet with three pastors separately, which is not unusual for me. I meet pastors in gyms, coffee shops, restaurants, and various other locations. I enjoy investing in local pastors because they are important to me and because pastors are my neighbors.

Whether you are on probation or a pastor, you are a neighbor whom God has called me to love. Who is in your neighborhood?

The original command to love our neighbors is found in Leviticus: "Do not take revenge or bear a grudge against members of your community, but love your neighbor as yourself; I am the LORD" (Lev. 19:18). Everyone we engage with today needs help. They need the gospel, or they need some encouragement. Everyone God puts in our path is our neighbor.

Leviticus 19 is a mini-commentary for all of the Ten Commandments. It is the only time God tells Moses to speak directly to the entire Israelite community. In this all-hands-on-deck message, Moses shows them how to live out their faith at home, at work, and in their neighborhoods. He teaches them how to love both the poor and the rich, the young and the old, the citizens and the immigrants.

The command to love our neighbors is in Leviticus, which is nowhere near the Shema (Deuteronomy). It was elevated to prominence by Jesus as the second greatest command in the whole Bible.

Jesus intends for our affections to go beyond our vertical love for God to extend to a horizontal love for all people. Both family and foreigners can expect to receive from us the same sacrificial, unilateral love we received from God. As Christians, we are called to help anyone in need, regardless of whether they can or will love us back. Pastors are called to rally our people to serve a global God in the context of our local community, where everyone has a universal need for love.

OUR NEEDIEST NEIGHBORS

A wake-up call came to me while pastoring Second Baptist Church in Conway, Arkansas. Several of our members were going door to door to invite people to the Easter services at our downtown campus, as well as the helicopter egg drop at our new west campus. The historic downtown campus was in an economically depressed housing community. Almost all of those downtown neighbors were polite and accepted the modest Easter gift bag we gave them. But as I walked off one of their porches, this haunting thought invaded my mind:

They aren't coming.

The dark reality set in for me. Our neediest neighbors weren't going to drive four miles to our other 50-acre campus to watch a helicopter drop plastic eggs filled with candy and prizes. I doubt many of them even owned a car.

Thousands of cheerful parents and children showed up every year from our city to see this pastel spectacle. Each of those would hear the gospel before they left. However, almost none of those who lived within the shadow of our downtown campus came to that pre-Easter event or our Sunday worship services.

My Great Commission bubble had burst, and my Great Commandment heart was broken. What kind of neighbors were we to those Jesus called us to love?

At that time, I had been preaching at the downtown campus for almost a decade. We had been completely ineffective at reaching our nearest and neediest neighbors for a very long time. The church continued to grow numerically, but it wasn't reaching those who lived in the neighborhood God put it in. We were inadvertently covering up our evangelical ineffectiveness primarily by transfer growth from those who would drive into the community each Sunday morning.

To make matters worse, we were relocating to a new, beautifully wooded campus that was literally ten times the size of our downtown campus. Initially, we put our downtown campus up for sale and planned on using those funds to pay for our new buildings. "For Sale" signs were up on every corner of our downtown property for about a year.

In the name of "stewardship" we were abandoning the neighborhood God had sovereignly placed us in . . . until one of our deacons asked me a simple question:

What if we don't sell the church?

It was a $4 million-dollar question asked by respected deacon, Dr. Dwight Davis. Dwight was the chairman of the Relocation Steering Committee, so he knew full well that our church was counting on the sale of that downtown campus to help pay for our new one.

We were attempting to solve a space problem, and the new campus was going to solve that challenge for years to come. Plus, it bordered a middle school and the University of Central Arkansas—the second largest college in Arkansas. The new campus would position us for new growth in a new community among new people.

But it also left behind a lot of old neighbors who needed the gospel.

Dwight is a pharmacist, so initially I suspected he had been self-medicating. Or perhaps he knew how to count pills better than dollar bills. I thought about telling Dwight to back off and leave the vision to rock star pastors like me. But by God's grace, I heard him out.

Dwight had just returned from his first international mission trip, and he was seeing his local neighbors in a different light. It was a light that needed to shine in my own dark heart. His new perspective came from taking a front-row seat in the global mission field. Now, Dwight saw his home church sitting in a field that was ready for harvest.

Jesus told his disciples, "Open your eyes and look at the fields, because they are ready for harvest" (John 4:35). It was a call to love and engage the present community without avoidance. If you'll remember the context, Jesus teaches us this right after he met a sinful Samaritan woman at a well. Even his own disciples thought he shouldn't be talking to her.

Dwight and I dreamed out loud that day about what kind of ministries could benefit the downtown community: food, clothes, medicine, dental, and an urban church. I had clearly been ambushed by God and a deacon! As a son of a deacon, I should have seen that coming. There was no turning back from

Dwight's compelling vision. When we shared the idea with our whole church family, they immediately loved it and responded with spontaneous applause.

We took our downtown campus off the market and saw giving increase immediately. We organized a city-wide alliance and created the Conway Ministry Center, which at the time of this writing hosts a dozen compassion ministries and two multi-ethnic church plants.

Jesus repeatedly taught and modeled for his disciples how to care for the poor (Matt. 19:21; Mark 12:42–43; Luke 4:18; 6:20; 11:41; 12:33; 14:13). God's Word is not silent about how to treat immigrants, prisoners, and those of different ethnicities. He made provision for both the poor and the foreign resident by forbidding farmers from gleaning after the reapers. Jesus's own ancestor Ruth was an immigrant who benefitted from God's people caring for the outsider and the poor (Ruth 2:1–6).

God has always loved our most dependent neighbors. He cares for those in financial need, family need, widows, and orphans. He also expects us to look out for those born with physical or mental handicaps. The Old Testament teaches, "Do not curse the deaf or put a stumbling block in front of the blind, but you are to fear your God; I am the Lord" (Lev. 19:14).

God also has much to say about how we do business with our neighbors. Honesty is expected of both the buyer and the seller, boss and employee; because at the end of the day, every business decision is a spiritual decision (Prov. 11:1; 16:11; 20:10, 23).

GREAT COMMANDMENT LOVE

Great Commandment pastors will do more than preach about their neediest neighbors. They will personally love them between Sundays and lead their churches to do the same. Pastors who see people as interruptions should be concerned that their calling has been replaced by lesser things. When necessary, we must admit that we are living in the wrong part of the parable of the Good Samaritan. When we find ourselves as the dismissive priest or the Levite, it's time to renew our love for our neighbor.

Our heart for the needy reveals something critical about our heart for God and his calling to lead. Would you be willing to show up late for a ministry appointment to help someone God drops into your life? Would you let a mission-minded member derail or slow down your building project or other ambitious goal? The needs of our neighbors are not a problem to push off, but they are signs of people who need to be embraced.

Our Lost Neighbors

This year Janet and I moved to Frisco, Texas, which is the home of the Dallas Cowboys and the new home of the PGA. Frisco is a fun place to live and is the fastest growing city in the United States.[1]

Frisco is also the most ethnically diverse city I have ever lived in. Although I graduated from a predominately black high school (John Tyler) and pastored in a predominately Hispanic neighborhood in south San Antonio, I have never lived among so many Asian Indians until now. Frisco is 50 percent white, 26 percent Asian, 11 percent Hispanic, 9 percent black, and 4 percent other.[2]

Indians are predominately Hindu, and in general have been more difficult to connect with than my most of my white, black, or Hispanic neighbors from previous neighborhoods. When I jog through our Frisco neighborhood two to three times a week, I wave and smile and sometimes talk to our neighbors. I am not only praying for their hearts, but my own heart as well because I want to love them genuinely and hopefully share the gospel with them. My personal struggle to be a Great Commandment/Great Commission neighbor is very real and very important to me.

We started this book focused on being a friend of God, and we will end it by focusing on being a friend of sinners. If our first love is Jesus, then we will love those he loves.

Jesus was intentional about building bridges to those whom others overlooked or looked down on. Sinners and social outcasts seemed to have a special place in the heart of Jesus. And more than just knowing something about them, he hung out with them regularly enough to be identified as their *friend*.

Our motivation for evangelism must be rooted in the love of God or our evangelistic fires will burn out quickly. We know what God has done in us and for us. So we know that mere will-power can never sustain us. Paul said, "Christ's love compels us" (2 Cor. 5:14 HCSB).

Great Commandment love translates into Great Commission initiatives when we start praying for unsaved and unchurched people by name. Our prayers will translate into gospel conversations because both the heart of the evangelist and the heart of those evangelized are being primed simultaneously through prayer.

The members of your church need to know that you are evangelizing the lost for many reasons. Not the least among them is that most believers have never shared the gospel. Sixty percent of evangelical Christians admit they have not told someone they didn't know about Jesus in the previous six months—57 percent have not with a non-Christian friend or loved one.[3] Yet the lost are all around us.

Only 1 out of 2 people in my dad's Builder generation attend church every week. Only 1 out of 3 people in my Gen X generation attend church every week. Only 1 out of 4 people in my children's generation attend church every week. This is not an encouraging trend! Most people in America claim to be Christian, but most professing Christians will not be in church this Sunday. Are the unchurched in our community uninterested or just uninvited?[4]

We have become a post-church society. Pastors need to stop shaking our fists at sinners and start pointing them to the Lamb of God who takes away the sins of the world. We are not just called to cast visions for evangelistic systems and devise witty church slogans. Loving our lost neighbors must be a personal priority, which means we will take up the Great Commission in our own neighborhoods.

Pastor, can you name every neighbor you can see from your front porch? If not, you have a great place to start because it is hard to love our neighbors if we do not know who they are!

LOVING OUR GLOBAL NEIGHBORS

Any evangelical would agree that loving our neighbors means reaching all the nations with the gospel, but have you ever tried to wrap your mind around how many global neighbors we actually have? The United Nations says there are approximately 7.5 billion people living on our planet, with that number growing to 11.2 billion by 2100.[5]

Am I supposed to love them all or just the 330 million neighbors in my native United States? The United States is becoming more global each day, having more people groups than every other nation except China and India. Both of those countries have about a billion more residents each than the United States does, so it is neither prudent nor biblical to spend all our resources and energies at home.

If your heart is hard toward the lost and the hurting, confess it as the sin it is. Ask God to help you be compelled by the love of Christ. If you are like Jonah and are running from God's assignment, stop. Let him recommission you and renew your Great Commandment love for your local and global neighbors.

God was successful in changing Jonah's hard heart, which means there is also hope for lethargic, angry, and rebellious ministers like us. God also changed the hearts of the barbaric Ninevites, which means there is hope for our gnarliest neighbors. God calls Christians to be missionaries who will enthusiastically "go" wherever he sends us.

Pastors and leaders are often the mobilizers, but that doesn't mean you can't be the mobilized. Laziness, apathy, and racism must have no part in how we see our global neighbors—and the nations.

Abraham was called to bless the nations, as were his descendants. It was and still is a tall order for Israel, considering the neighborhood God sent them into. The church is made up of Abraham's spiritual descendants who live under the same call to bless the nations. From early in the church's work, the Holy Spirit sent them to people unlike them both ethnically and culturally.

Philip was a deacon and the first leader in the New Testament to break through the wall of ethnicity to share the gospel. Peter eventually followed Philip's lead after God visited him in a dream. James's letter on maturing a Christian puts down a principle that can lead us to do the same. He wrote, "If you fulfill the royal law prescribed in the Scripture, 'Love your neighbor as yourself,' you are doing well. If, however, you show favoritism, you commit sin and are convicted by the law as transgressors" (James 2:8–9).

Consider these questions:

- Do you have any friends who do not look or talk like you?
- Do you have any friends who do not believe like you?
- Do you have any friends who do not vote like you?

You and I can love your earthly neighbors without loving our heavenly Father, but you cannot love our heavenly Father without loving our earthly neighbors.

OUR HATEFUL NEIGHBORS

Sometimes the spiritual underdog we are called to love will try to bite us.

You know what I'm talking about. Jesus not only expanded the demographics of our neighborhood to include foreigners, but also our enemies.

> "You have heard that it was said, 'Love your neighbor and hate your enemy.' But I tell you, love your enemies and pray for those who persecute you, so that you may be children of your Father in heaven. For he causes his sun to rise on the evil and the good, and sends rain on the righteous and the unrighteous. For if you love

those who love you, what reward will you have?
Don't even the tax collectors do the same? And
if you greet only your brothers and sisters, what
are you doing out of the ordinary? Don't even
the Gentiles do the same?" (Matt. 5:43–47)

It is a radical shift from the conventional Hebrew interpreta-
tion of *love your neighbor*. The new standard bucked just about
every cultural norm and still does.

A pastor once told me about an ornery church member who
has written him dozens of long, anonymous letters. This critic
saw fit to copy the rest of the church members as well. He literally claimed to have the gift of criticism, which seems more like
a curse to me.

No matter what church you serve in or what leadership position you hold, you will eventually be criticized. You will be hurt
by people you have invested in and loved deeply. It happened to
Paul, and it will happen to you. It can be especially traumatic for
young pastors because they are less likely to have their guard up
when someone takes a swing at them.

Seek reconciliation first. If your church has a long history of
treating their pastors like piñatas, find a new church. If you are a
lay leader, you don't have to like your pastor, but you do have to
love and respect him. Be careful not to make your current pastor
pay for something that your former pastor did.

For the sake of the kingdom, don't participate in an ongoing
feud with your faith family. Not only will the believers lose, but

the unbelievers will lose as well. It hinders growth and harms Christ's good reputation. In the face of thorny people, Jesus expected us to love.

> "I give you a new command: Love one another. Just as I have loved you, you are also to love one another. By this everyone will know that you are my disciples, if you love one another." (John 13:34–35)

Love is how the lost world knows that we belong to Christ and tells them something about him. Hatred on the other hand has a foothold on a lot of Christians, which is repelling lost people from our churches. Unforgiveness is unforgiveable according to Jesus: "If you don't forgive people, your Father will not forgive your wrongdoing" (Matt. 6:15 HCSB). It is a shockingly strong statement from the Sermon on the Mount.

In 1 John 2 we learn that those who hate their spiritual brothers and sisters are liars who live in darkness. One thing we all have in common is a need for God's grace, both for our neighbors and ourselves. No matter who it is or how they seek to mistreat you, love them. They may reject you or the church. They may tragically reject Jesus, but we are still called to love our enemies.

A GREAT COMMANDMENT LEADER

Have you ever met a Great Commission pastor who was not also a Great Commandment pastor? I have met plenty, and they sure are hard to get along with. These task-oriented leaders love to boast about buildings, budgets, and baptisms. They love to talk about missions, discipleship, and expanding the kingdom. All commendable objectives unless they are pursued without the essential ingredient of love.

How about vice versa? **Have you ever met a Great Commandment pastor who was not also a Great Commission pastor?** I cannot think of one. Great Commandment pastors will invariably lead Great Commission lives and ministries because they are compelled by their love for God and their neighbors.

In the next and final chapter, we will explore how the Great Commandments and Great Commission complement one another in our daily lives and ministries.

You've read it before, but read the Great Commission again. But this time, do so with the Great Commandment love in mind.

> "Go, therefore, and make disciples of all nations, baptizing them in the name of the Father and of the Son and of the Holy Spirit, teaching them to observe everything I have commanded you. And remember, I am with you always, to the end of the age." (Matt. 28:19–20)

If I am going all-in for God, then I will eventually be going all-out with the gospel. How can we possibly keep all of that amazing grace and love for ourselves?

Take some time right now to let the Holy Spirit assess your heart for the world. Be ready to lay it all on the line. Pastoring from start to finish means accepting our mission to love our neighbors in every place God sends us. So let's get our "yes" on the table and let God put the assignment in front of us.

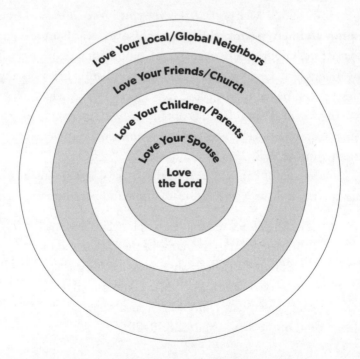

CHAPTER 12

ASSESS AND APPLY

The Greatest Commandment has called us back to your first love with unflinching abandon. My prayer is that your love for Jesus has been rekindled somewhat by reading this book and allowing the Holy Spirit to penetrate your heart afresh.

The second greatest commandment is likewise a clarion call to love. We will love those who Jesus loves—starting with our nearest neighbors. You would not have read this far if you were not interested in growing your love for both God and your neighbors.

Thank you for investing your time in this journey with me. Your desire to lead well from start to finish is commendable! I would be honored to hear what God is doing in your life and ministry. You can connect with me on just about every social media channel by searching for @markdance. I also would be honored to send you encouraging blog posts every other week if you subscribe for free at markdance.net.

As we wrap up this book, I want to give you a thirty-day challenge that is intended to help you assess and improve your Great Commandment/Commission relationships.

Once you know how you're doing, you can strive to be more intentional by setting specific relationship goals. Rather than just moving on to the next book or study, stop and ask God to show you how to apply the most important commandments in Scripture to your life right now. If you take this first step today, then you will have given no room for apathy to set in on the Great Commandment life and Great Commission ministry that you aspire to have.

The following self-assessment and application are brief, but very important to bringing the second commandment home.

OUR FAMILY NEIGHBORHOOD

How would you know if your love for your biological or nuclear family is growing? Is there evidence in your calendar of investing time with your family? Write down at least one practical way you can connect with each immediate family member in the next thirty days. Make a secret date night with your spouse within this thirty-day window.

_____

_____

> If anyone does not know how to manage his
> own household, how will he take care of God's
> church? (1 Tim. 3:5)

OUR FRIENDSHIP NEIGHBORHOOD

Perhaps Satan's most effective scheme is isolation. When he isolates his enemies—us—then we become defensive and selfish.

No one ever does well fighting alone. But we get confused because we love iconic characters like James Bond, Rambo, and Batman. Superheroes go charging into battle alone, and we cheer for them. When you and I go into battle alone, Satan is the only one cheering. Even superheroes fight better together (e.g., Avengers, Justice League, Fellowship of the Ring, Dallas Cowboys—sorry, I got carried away).

My point is this: when we get isolated, we get weak. It's when the temptations of power, gluttony, lust, and all sorts of addictive behaviors come screaming at us.

Three more important results from the Pastors' Spouse Survey are cause for concern:

- 1 out of 10 spouse can count on a church friend a great deal.
- 7 out of 10 have very few to confide in about important matters.
- 1 out of 3 pastors feel isolated.[1]

Since life and ministry are too hard to do alone, I want to encourage you to reject the notion that ministry is a sentence to solitary confinement. We preach and teach that Christian brothers need to have healthy fellowship. But far too often, we distance ourselves. We must seek friendships both among other church leaders and our neighbors. If you don't have a close friend in your life, look first in your own church.

Who is your best friend, and when is the last time you talked? Write below your closest friends' names and one way you can connect with them this month.

_____

_____

OUR GLOBAL NEIGHBORHOOD

God calls all his followers to become missionaries. No sooner had Jesus called his disciples to "come" to him, than he commissioned them to "go" and make disciples. If our members are undertrained and under-challenged, there is nobody to blame but ourselves.

According to Ephesians 4:12, if we are not equipping the saints, we are enabling them. But more than completing programs is needed. We need our hearts changed so that we can help see their hearts changed. It is time to ask God to fill you with his love for the nations.

At the end of the day, we can only take our church to places we are willing to go. If your love for your unchurched and unsaved friends has grown cold, would you consider taking the time to rekindle that fire? Write down one way you will pursue a friendship with someone who is unsaved or unchurched this month.

PRESS ON!

My prayer is that this book has been a journey of grace for you. A guilt trip would be a failure and would only have a temporary impact on your life and ministry. So if you feel conviction, then let the Holy Spirit finish his work so that you can finish your race strong. If we finish well, it will be because of the same grace of God by which we started.

Serving as a pastor, missionary, or ministry leader is the most mind-blowing, heart-expanding, grace-living adventure we can fathom. It is an amazing thought that the King of the universe would call us to the task of leading his people to grow in their love for him and fulfill his mission on the earth. But he has. And so, we will.

> My purpose is to finish my course and the ministry I received from the Lord Jesus. (Acts 20:24)

Paul's final words in writing to this same ministry team serve as a sacred model for how to finish well in ministry:

> The time for my departure is close. I have fought the good fight, I have finished the race, I have kept the faith. There is reserved for me the crown of righteousness, which the Lord, the righteous Judge, will give me on that day, and not only to me, but to all those who have loved his appearing. (2 Tim. 4:6–8)

NOTES

Introduction

1. Tom Bowman, "Major Combat in Iraq Over, Bush Declares," *Baltimore Sun*, May 2, 2003, https://www.baltimoresun.com/bal-te.bush-02may02-story.html.

2. Tim Peters, "10 Real Reasons Pastors Quit Too Soon," ChurchLeaders, April 6, 2018, https://churchleaders.com/pastors/pastor-articles/161343-tim_peters_10_common_reasons_pastors_quit_too_soon.html?utm_content=buffer99dde&utm_medium=social&utm_source=facebook.com&utm_campaign=buffer&fbclid=IwAR1l_jRMMzJREgkwxLyKnF-Q89PVsnR7H6fvBXtHkgaThx.

3. "Study of Pastor Attrition and Pastoral Ministry," Lifeway Research, accessed October 13, 2022, https://research.lifeway.com/pastorprotection/.

4. "Few Pastors Left the Pulpit Despite Increased Pressure," Lifeway Research, October 25, 2021, https://research.lifeway.com/2021/10/25/few-pastors-left-the-pulpit-despite-increased-pressure/.

Chapter 1: The Main Thing

1. The origin of this saying is Stephen Covey, author of *The 7 Habits of Highly Effective People*.

2. Bill Bright, *First Love: Renewing Your Passion for God* (Union City, CA: New Life Publications: 2002), 19.

3. David Ferguson, *The Great Commandment Principle* (1998; rev. ed., Cedar Park, TX: Relationship Press: 2013), 9.

4. Former UCLA college basketball coach John Wooden.

Chapter 2: A 4D Love

1. See un.org.

Chapter 3: With All My Heart

1. Brian Croft and Jim Savastio, *The Pastor's Soul: The Call and Care of an Undershepherd* (County Durham, UK: Evangelical Press: 2018).

2. David Kinnaman and Gabe Lyons, *Good Faith: Being a Christian When Society Thinks You're Irrelevant and Extreme* (Grand Rapids: Baker, 2016).

3. "Letter to My Younger Self," *The Players' Tribune*, November 1, 2016, https://www.theplayerstribune.com/articles/ray-allen-letter-to-my-younger -self.

Chapter 4: With All My Soul

1. Lindsey Bever, "Woman Wakes Up in Morgue. The 'Lazarus Phenomenon' Surfaces More Than You Think," *Washington Post*, November 17, 2014, https://www.washingtonpost.com/news/morning-mix/wp/2014/11/17 /woman-wakes-up-in-morgue-the-lazarus-phenomenon-surfaces-more -than-you-think/.

2. John Ortberg, *Soul Keeping: Caring for the Most Important Part of You* (Grand Rapids: Zondervan, 2014), 164.

3. Dave Johnson in "Leader's Insight: The High Price of Dying (to Self)," *Christianity Today*, Spring 2007, https://www.christianitytoday.com /pastors/2007/april-online-only/cln70416.html.

4. Jane G. Goldberg, "Psychoanalysis: A Treatment of the Soul," *Huffington Post*, August 26, 2011, https://www.huffpost.com/entry /psychoanalysis-freud-history_b_904139.

Chapter 5: With All My Mind

1. Matt Bloom, *Flourishing in Ministry: How to Cultivate Clergy Wellbeing* (Lanham, MD: Rowman & Littlefield, 2019), 7.

2. Aaron Earls, "Pastors Have Congregational and, for Some, Personal Experience with Mental Illness," Lifeway Research, August 2, 2022, https://research.lifeway.com/2022/08/02/pastors-have-congregational-and-for-some-personal-experience-with-mental-illness/.

3. Scott Barkley, "GuideStone Expands Focus on Helping Pastors Start Well, Finish Better," Kentucky Today, July 23, 2022, https://www.kentucky today.com/baptist_life/guidestone-expands-focus-on-helping-pastors-start-well-finish-better/article_17811cd6-0a8a-11ed-8c0d-3b5dbae94bbc.html.

4. "Pastor Protection Research Survey," March 2015, https://research .lifeway.com/wp-content/uploads/2015/08/Pastor-Protection-Quantitative -Report-Final.pdf.

5. "Study of Acute Mental Illness and Christian Faith," May 2014, http://research.lifeway.com/wp-content/uploads/2014/09/Acute-Mental -Illness-and-Christian-Faith-Research-Report-1.pdf.

6. Paul David Tripp, *Dangerous Calling: Confronting the Unique Challenges of Pastoral Ministry* (Wheaton, IL: Crossway, 2012), 21.

Chapter 6: With All My Strength

1. Elisabeth Elliot, ed., *Journals of Jim Elliot* (1978; repr., Grand Rapids: Revell, 2002), 174.

2. Chuck Norris, *Against All Odds: My Story* (Nashville: B&H Publishing Group, 2004), 245.

3. "Overweight and Obesity Statistics," National Institute of Diabetes and Digestive and Kidney Diseases, last reviewed September 2021, https://www.niddk.nih.gov/health-information/health-statistics/overweight-obesity; https://www.cdc.gov/obesity/data/adult.html.

4. "Assessing Your Weight and Health Risk," National Heart, Lung, and Blood Institute, accessed October 14, 2022, https://www.nhlbi.nih.gov/health/educational/lose_wt/risk.htm.

5. "Top 10 Things to Know about the Second Edition of the Physical Activity Guidelines for Americans," Health.gov, accessed October 14, 2022, https://health.gov/our-work/nutrition-physical-activity/physical-activity-guidelines/current-guidelines/top-10-things-know.

6. David Frost, *Billy Graham: Candid Conversations with a Public Man* (Colorado Springs: David C Cook, 2014), 181.

7. "Why We Don't Take Vacation," *Time*, July 11, 2016, https://time.com/4389139/why-dont-we-take-vacation/.

8. *Christian Counseling Today*, vol. 10, no. 3, 2002.

Chapter 7: Assess and Apply

1. The term *halo effect* (a.k.a. "halo error") was first introduced into psychological-research circles in 1920 in a paper authored by Edward Thorndike titled *A Constant Error in Psychological Ratings*.

Chapter 8: Who Is My Neighbor?

1. Cara Buckley, "Man Is Rescued by Stranger on Subway Tracks," *New York Times*, January 3, 2007, https://www.nytimes.com/2007/01/03/nyregion/03life.html.

2. Kathryn Spink, *Mother Teresa: An Authorized Biography* (New York: HarperOne, 2011).

Chapter 9: My Family Neighborhood

1. "Pastor Spouse Research Study," August 2017, http://research.lifeway.com/wp-content/uploads/2017/09/Pastor-Spouse-Research-Report-Sept-2017.pdf.

2. Peter Scazzero, *The Emotionally Healthy Leader: How Transforming Your Inner Life Will Deeply Transform Your Church, Team, and the World* (Grand Rapids: Zondervan, 2015), 92.

3. Charles H. Spurgeon sermon, "The Heavenly Race," New Park Street Chapel, June 11, 1858, www.spurgeon.org/resource-library/sermons/the-heavenly-race#flipbook/.

4. Charlotte Alter, "Paul Ryan's Demand for Time with Family Prompts Hypocrisy Charges," *Time*, October 21, 2015, https://time.com/4081956/paul-ryan-house-speaker-race-republicans-congress-family-leave/.

5. Shana Lebowitz, "Paul Ryan Says He's Retiring to Stop Being a 'Weekend Dad,'" BuinessInsider.com, April 11, 2018, https://www.businessinsider.com/paul-ryan-retiring-to-spend-time-with-family-2018-4.

6. "Lifeway Research 2017 Survey of American Pastor's Spouses," Lifeway Research, accessed October 17, 2022, http://research.lifeway.com/wp-content/uploads/2017/09/Pastor-Spouse-Quantitative-Long-Report-2017.pdf.

Chapter 10: My Friendship Neighborhood

1. Sheena McKenzie, "British Explorer Henry Worsley Dies Crossing Antarctic 30 Miles Short of Goal," CNN, January 25, 2016, https://www.cnn.com/2016/01/25/world/henry-worsley-explorer-dies-antarctic.

Chapter 11: Our Global Neighborhood

1. Than Merrill, "Top 10 Fastest Growing Cities in the US," Updated 2022, https://www.fortunebuilders.com/fastest-growing-cities-in-the-us/.

2. "Frisco at a Glance 2021," Frisco, accessed October 18, 2022, https://www.friscotexas.gov/DocumentCenter/View/4900/2021_At-A-Glance-PDF?bidId=.

3. "Christians Say They Are Seeking but They Aren't Having Evangelistic Conversations," Lifeway Research, May 24, 2022, https://research.lifeway.com/2022/05/24/christians-say-theyre-seeking-but-not-having-evangelistic-conversations/.

4. "The State of the Church 2016," Barna, September 15, 2016, https://www.barna.com/research/state-church-2016/.

5. "World Population Projected to Reach 9.8 Billion in 2050, and 11.2 Billion in 2100," United Nations, accessed October 18, 2022, https://www.un.org/en/desa/world-population-projected-reach-98-billion-2050-and-112-billion-2100#:~:text=COVID%2D19-,World%20population%20projected%20to%20reach%209.8%20billion%20in%202050%2C%20and,Nations%20report%20being%20launched%20today.

Chapter 12: Assess and Apply

1. Bob Smietana, "Pastor's Spouses Experience Mixed Blessings," Lifeway Research, September 12, 2017, https://research.lifeway.com/2017/09/12/pastors-spouses-experience-mixed-blessings/.

At GuideStone®, our vision is that **every servant of Christ finishes well.**

 Retirement

 Insurance

 Faith-Based Investing

 **Mission:Dignity®**

GuideStone.org
1-888-98-GUIDE (1-888-984-8433)